LOST SEOUL

Lost Seoul

Cover design and illustration by Kimberly Porter

Book design by Andrea Klosterman Harris

All interior illustrations and photos by Jin S. Stearns

ISBN 978-1-300-80864-0

First Trade Edition

To Kim Tae Hee and Ahn Kyu Soo, who gave me life, and

Frank and Patricia Stearns, who made it worth living

Foreword

This book was a long time in the making; over a lifetime, to be exact. I cannot express how grateful I am to the many people who helped it come together. Thank you to my wife Carolyn who listened patiently to my narrations at all odd hours of the day and night, and put them into words in a way I could never do; to my sister-in-law, Andrea Klosterman Harris, who donated countless hours editing and critiquing each chapter with insight and humor as only she could do; Kimberly Porter for the magnificent cover artwork; the people at Holt who gave me a forum to present this; and to everyone in my Korean and American families, of whom I am so proud to call family. Instead of a tragedy, I hope the reader will see my story as one of triumph, as I do.

Happy reading!

Chapter 1

Busan, South Korea 1968

My name is Kim Ji Soo.[1] This is my story.

I really don't remember what my parents looked like. They were out of my life before I could get a clear memory imprinted in my six-year-old mind. What I do remember is that we were very poor, pretty much like the rest of the village, but my two older brothers and I were very close. Kyang Soo was the oldest at around ten, and Yae Soo was in the middle, close to eight. We played together every day, which included climbing up to the mountain top, swimming in the ocean, fighting with the neighbor kids, or whatever fun there was to be had right at the moment.

We lived in a small village in the larger city of Busan, on the most southeastern tip of South Korea. We were nestled in an area surrounded by mountains and the ocean. The year was 1968, and the village where we lived was very simple and quiet. It was not anything like the busy metropolis that Busan has become today, as the second largest city in

---

1. In Asian culture, your surname is first, then your first name, then your middle name.

South Korea. We lived plainly, as did most of the people in the village.

The Korean War between North and South Korea had ended a little over a decade earlier, and the country was trying to settle back into one of peace again. During the war, Busan had become a refugee camp site as it was only one of two cities in South Korea not captured by North Korea. While the population rose to over one million people, the area where we lived was still quite rural.

* * *

I remember we lived in a one room house. There was a kitchen, bedroom and living room all in one. It was a round house made out of straw and clay. There was a makeshift door made of sticks woven together. Most houses back then did not have windows that you could open to get fresh air when it was hot, or close when it was too cold. The window we had in our house was just a small square hole; there was no glass or frame. When it got too cold, we would board it up with straw to keep some of the cold air from blowing in.

I don't especially remember exactly how I learned Mom and Dad were gone since I was very small at the time. One day they were no longer there at the house, and for some reason, I can remember the house vividly, but not my parents' faces. However, what I did recall was a lot of arguing between them. I was not very upset that they were gone because I didn't really understand what "gone" meant. The permanency and gravity of the situation didn't really sink in until I was much older.

I do remember it was fall, because the air had begun to turn colder. It was often windy and chilly, and the leaves were coming down slowly. Even though the house was not much, it was a place for us to stay warm against the whipping winds and chilly air. Kyang Soo thought our parents would come back soon to be with us again, but until then, he told Yae Soo and me that we must stay together as a family. It was so important to him that we not be separated. I really didn't know what was going on; why had they left us, and who would do such a thing to a family? These are questions that ran through my mind for many, many years.

Kyang Soo had to bear all the responsibility as the caretaker for us. How overwhelmed he must have felt at only ten years old, just a kid himself ...

* * *

Every day, Kyang Soo would go outside and be gone for a little while. What was so great was that he'd come back with food. We didn't know how he did it, but we loved him for it. The food that he got in the morning needed to last us all day, so we would have to watch how much we'd eat, and save what we could. It was the same with water. The food was nothing more than rice and sometimes a bit of boiled vegetable, but to three starving kids, it was a gourmet meal. We were focused on survival; either eat or die of starvation. We didn't even have chopsticks, so we ate hungrily with what we had—our hands. The rice was not in bowls; it was just set onto a flat clay stone. On the days that people gave Kyang Soo rice still in small mesh potato sacks, we would eat it right from there, each impatiently taking turns at a small scoop to sustain us. Since we had no furniture, we would just sit on the hard clay floors.

By now, winter was drawing closer, so Kyang Soo had to also gather sticks and twigs to build a small fire beside the house to keep us from freezing. I remember he would go outside and gather wood to build the fire. I can still picture his light blonde hair sticking out like a sore thumb in contrast to the dimly lit sky as he gathered the sticks. It was so unusual for a Korean child to have such light hair, as it was a natural Asian trait to have dark hair and dark eyes. Yae Soo and I were both dark haired, and Kyang Soo was the only one whose hair was so fair. That is what I can remember the most about him, besides his unwavering drive to take care of us.

He would get large rocks and put them into the fire. After a few minutes of heating them in the fire, he would take those hot rocks and bring them into the house to keep us warm. That felt really nice. The clay floors, although hard and uncomfortable, were designed to retain and spread the heat from the fire so that we could stay warm on the cold and often sunless days.

We would wear the same clothes, just adding more layers as the weather turned colder. We used our shirts as hats by pulling them over our heads and tying the sleeves at the back to keep warm. This is how we and many others lived in the village: a very basic and simple life. Kyang Soo went around the village to beg for any extra scraps of clothing people could spare. We ended up with some empty potato sacks that doubled for us as both coats and blankets, depending on our needs at the moment.

Although I was too young to understand at the time, I am not sure how the villagers felt when they knew we were alone and struggling to care for ourselves. My guess is that they were also struggling themselves, yet they did their best to provide what they could to at least help us survive.

It didn't matter what was the weather; rain or shine, Kyang Soo was out every day visiting from house to house. He would always make sure Yae Soo and I would eat first, saving some food later for himself. He always put us before himself. He never said anything bad about our parents, or about other people, and would always encourage us to stay positive. This went on for several days, then months.

* * *

We had to learn everything quickly in Korea, and at a young age. I think maybe that aspect of the culture was what helped save us back then, along with a big handful of God looking out for us. To have to take care of your basic needs as a child was hard enough to comprehend, but what Kyang Soo was able to do in caring for his two younger siblings as well made him all the more incredible when I look back now. I cannot imagine how strong and brave he would have to have been to take on this responsibility at ten years old.

Each day was the same as the one before it, and at night the three of us would pray before going to sleep on the hard clay floor. We would all have to cuddle together as closely as possible to stay warm. Once the fire went out, we had to let it go, huddling together and relying on the warmth from the ashes, the burlap potato sacks and each other to keep us alive through the night.

Nights were the worst. Some nights it was so cold that nothing we did made any difference. We couldn't be huddled together any more closely than we already were.

We had to get enough body heat between us, shivering to sleep most of the time, and praying that we would wake to see another day.

I can't remember how many times I cried myself to sleep. I was pretty scared about what was going to happen with us, and if we would ever see our parents again.

Even just to wash our faces and bodies was a chore. With no running water, we would have to go down to the creek and wash and bath in the ice cold water. Even that was a hike. It wasn't just outside the house; it was at least a few hundred yards away.

Thus became our daily routine. Days turned into weeks, and weeks turned into months. Finally one day, Kyang Soo decided we must head out and either search for our parents or find relatives in a more distant village. He didn't have a plan, but he knew that there was nothing in the village anymore for us except the day to day struggle to survive. He must have felt strongly there was a reason or sign that we must leave, and that things were not going to be any easier if we stayed. I trusted that he knew what was best for us at the time. I may have lost a lot of hope in those early days of my life, but there was always one constant: my deep trust in Kyang Soo never wavered.

Chapter 2

The Journey to Nowhere

Kyang Soo did not have a real plan, but he did seem to have a feeling that it was right for us to go. We took what little we had: the clothes on our backs, any extra potato sacks we had managed to gather from the villagers, and a lot of matches. Kyang Soo knew that matches were a must-have item for us so we would not succumb to the bitter cold. They served as both heat and light to guide us on the way to only God knew where.

Kyang Soo led us as we walked from one small village to another throughout Busan. Some days it was a half-day journey to the next village; some days it was even longer. We stopped to rest at night. If we were too far away from the next village, we would stop in a nearby cornfield. Kyang Soo would chop down corn stalks for us to lie down on, and then chop down more to cover us up. As always, we would huddle together to keep warm. If our journey took us through the woods instead, we would search for an indentation in the ground to lie in at night. Oftentimes, it would be muddy or damp, but it still offered more protection from the cold and bitter night winds. Kyang Soo would gather twigs to cover us, and make a small fire to keep us safe and warm.

I am not proud to admit that we had to steal the corn from the cornfield, but when that was all we had to eat besides what meager rations we could beg from the kindhearted villagers as we passed through, it was what needed to be done. We did what we had to do to get by and just hoped to see another day. We would pass through rice fields and cornfields as we traveled along endless miles of dirt trails. The only guide we had was the sun in the daytime and the moon at night. We didn't know where we were headed, but we managed to stay brave. I can't remember feeling scared, even though it seems scary to me today when I think of three young boys struggling to survive and walking mile upon mile with no real destination in sight. I think we were too numb from trying to stay alive to let fear be a barrier to us.

At every village we passed through we would knock on doors. My brother would ask if anyone knew anything about our parents, and if they had any food to spare. The answer about the parents was always no, but most people managed to share a bit of what little they did have. Some people even let us stay the night on their clay floors, and in the morning we would thank them and continue on our way. Those times were a luxury for us, when we had warm water heated in an iron kettle to wash ourselves with, rather than the cold spring water we had become accustomed to.

I don't remember how long we traveled around Busan, possibly only a few short weeks, but somehow we ended up back at our house in our own village. We had still not found our parents and did not know what else to do.

* * *

A short time passed and somehow we ended up with a relative in Seoul, South Korea. My memory is fuzzy about how long we had been back and how we had gone to stay with the relative in Seoul. I don't know if a relative came looking for us eventually, and don't remember how we got to Seoul, but I know that I just did whatever Kyang Soo did. He was my protector and caretaker; I went wherever he did.

I remember not liking where we were staying in Seoul. Kyang Soo would come and go and not come back for several days at a time. I don't think he felt comfortable at that place, either. I don't recall how Yae Soo felt, but I wasn't happy. I think Kyang Soo felt like we were intruders and more of a burden to this family, and that feeling was rubbing off onto me. I got it into my head that I didn't want to stay there anymore, and became determined to do something about it.

Kyang Soo had gotten a job shining shoes at the nearby Seoul Train Station, a large hub where many people traveled around Korea day to day. His goal was to earn enough money shining shoes to buy three train tickets back to Busan so that we could at least be back in our familiar village. I think he may have heard some news about our mother and that she was back in Busan, so he wanted us to go back there again.

One morning, as Kyang Soo headed off to work, I stealthily followed behind him. I was so unhappy at the relatives' house, and all I wanted to do was go back home to Busan. I was young and naïve at six years old, and thought Kyang Soo would take care of me no matter where we lived. I don't think I appreciated how hard he struggled to take care of us back in Busan.

The train station was in Dongdae-moongu, Seoul City. It was a monstrous building of brick and stone, with a domed roof over the center of the building, and long hallways extending out from all sides. I had never seen anything like it in all of my life. It was crowded; people rushing here and there, getting on and off trains, everyone in a mad scramble to get where they needed to be. There were more people in one area than I had ever experienced, and the noise and chaos was overwhelming to me.

As Kyang Soo entered the front doors, I snuck up beside him so he could see me. He was startled that I was there. I don't remember much of what was said between us, but he became angry that I followed him. He was in a hurry to get to his job, and I was in the way. He said I needed to go home. As he walked away, I got scared. More and more people got in between us, and soon I couldn't see him anymore. I spotted a bench in the corner nearby and crawled under it to hide. I hoped that Kyang Soo would come back and get me and show me the way back home. It was almost as if I was invisible to the throngs of people, because no one stopped to help; they just kept hurrying by as if I was not even there.

* * *

I am not sure how long I stayed that way, but to me, it seemed like hours. Finally I got up. I didn't have a choice. I was lost and hungry, and no one was paying any attention to me. I needed food, but without my brothers there to help, I did not know what to do. I saw other boys shining people's shoes with a cloth and getting a few coins in return. I thought that was how I could get money for food.

It was pretty simple, really. Back then you just spit on the shoe and shined with the cloth. That is literally what they meant by a "spit shine." I quickly made enough to buy a small bit of food from one of the vendors close to the station. Exhausted and scared, I slept underneath the bench that night. All the while, I kept an eye on every passing face, always hoping it would be Kyang Soo or Yae Soo. It never was.

A couple of days passed by, but no one seemed to care that I was lost. Kyang Soo and my family did not come looking for me, and no one at the station took notice of yet another vagrant boy shining shoes.

I remember I was heading toward the vendors after a morning spent shining shoes and wandering around the station looking for my brothers when a strange man came along, grabbed my hand and started to lead me away. I was scared and tried to tell him that I was waiting for my brothers; that I just wanted to find my brothers. He said something along the lines of, "I know where they are and I will take you to them." When you are six- years old and someone tells you something like that, you are more than willing to believe it. As we were walking, he gave me a small bit of food to eat. I had no choice but to follow him. The fact that he was holding onto me pretty tightly made it clear that I could not run away.

My life's journey had begun, and would soon take me far away from the brothers I loved dearly, and upon whom I had completely depended.

Chapter 3

My First Orphanage

The man turned out to be someone who finds stray kids and sells them to the highest bidder. Usually these people would try to sell them to shady orphanages. Their goal was to sell you to an orphanage for money, then that orphanage would try to turn around and sell you through adoption, or to another orphanage. Younger kids were ideal because when you hit ten years old, you were generally beyond the age that people wanted to adopt, and therefore became less profitable for the orphanages. If you were too old, and no longer "desirable," they didn't really care much where you went, just as long as they no longer had to support you. You were turned out onto the streets to fend for yourself. A proper orphanage would not take in a child unless he or she came through the police department or other children's home first. A passerby was not allowed to just bring in a child, but that is what happened to me.

He led me to a place I knew nothing about. There wasn't anything familiar to me, and my brothers were not there. It was an orphanage called Hwa Saeng Won, located in Kohyang County. There were several small one bedroom buildings, more like huts, that could each hold around twenty or so kids.

I was scared to be away from the train station because that was the last place where I had seen my brothers. I was afraid they would come back for me and I would not be there. I tried to tell the people at the orphanage this, but no one would listen to me, or seemed to care. I was just another child without a home that could potentially bring money to them if they could adopt me out. On May 12, 1969, I officially became an orphan in Hwa Saeng Won orphanage.

* * *

There were a lot of kids there, ranging from age three to almost ten years old. Kids were not really kept in the orphanage past age ten because there was just no room for them. After they "aged out", they were sent out to the streets to care for themselves, or rumored to be taken in by the state to be placed into the military.

Girls and boys of all ages shared the same room. They packed as many kids in one room as they could without much regard to gender or age. I don't remember much about the room except that it was cold and crowded and I did not want to be there. I would have given anything to once again be at the relative's house in Seoul, no matter how uncomfortable or unhappy I had been there. Even the cold nights spent wandering around Busan with Kyang Soo and Yae Soo would have been a welcome relief compared to the bleak surroundings I now faced.

If I knew at that moment that I would be living at Hwa Saeng Won for three long, hard years, I don't know that I would have had the strength to go on. I guess it was lucky after all that I had so much instability so far in my young life because I had learned to quickly adapt to any new situation. I was a survivor.

I was issued two sets of clothing, one that I wore, and another as a back-up to wear when I was washing the first set. It was my responsibility to keep them clean and wash them every week. There was only a plain shirt and pants. There weren't any underwear.

There was no running water in the place. All the water we used came from a creek. There were several creeks in the area, and the water came from the mountains close by. Some boys had the job of taking two buckets attached to a pole that went over their shoulders and making trip after trip to the creek to bring water to dump into the big round wooden tank centered in the middle of the orphanage. This was a central tank for everyone to use for drinking or cooking. The water tank was never used for washing clothes, but sometimes someone would take a bucket of water and dump it over us to wash us up. Otherwise, we were expected to bathe in the creek, no matter what the season. We ended up taking fewer bathes in the winter because it was much too cold.

When the clothes needed to be washed, we would take them down to the creek. We would dunk them in the cold water and beat them against the rocks to get the excess water out. We would let them air dry on a line, or lay them on rocks in the sun. If it was really cold out, we would put them by the fire.

The facilities were pretty basic. Since there was no indoor plumbing, we had to do our "business" outside as well. There was a special hole, around three or four feet deep, that we all used as the toilet. We placed two long narrow boards across the hole, with enough space between them for our waste to fall through as we sat on them. Because there was also no toilet paper, we had to use big wide leaves. Dry ones were no good; they would just crumble in our hands. The best ones that we all fought over to get were the ones freshly picked from the tree branch. Amazing when I think back how the taller, older boys could just reach higher to get the best choice!

There were no toothbrushes or toothpaste. We just had to crush up some rock salt and put it on our fingers and brush every day. In the wintertime, our hands usually got very dry and chapped, so pouring the rock salt onto our fingers then was pretty painful.

Months went by, and time cycled through summer, fall, winter and back again to spring. Over this period, I had been paired up with different older boys to learn how to work the different areas of the orphanage. You see, nothing was free; we had to work for everything. Just to live in the orphanage, we had to work to stay. No matter your age, you had a job to do.

Besides the job I mentioned earlier of getting water to fill the huge vat several times a day, there were many other jobs that we had to do. We had to gather smaller sticks and branches and give them to the older kids who were better able to carry them down the hillside back to the orphanage. They used a contraption that was similar to a camper's giant backpack. It was a large wooden A-frame rack onto which we neatly stacked twigs, branches and leaves. When it was full, we would secure the load by tying a rope over and under the pile so that it would all stay in place. Sometimes the pile of twigs could get really huge, over five or six feet high. Then an older boy would kneel down on one knee and put his arms through the rope armholes in the frame so that it nestled against his back and shoulders.

With all his might, he would pull himself back up onto his feet while balancing the load. A couple boys at a time would wear these "knapsacks" as they gradually made their way down the hillside back to the orphanage.

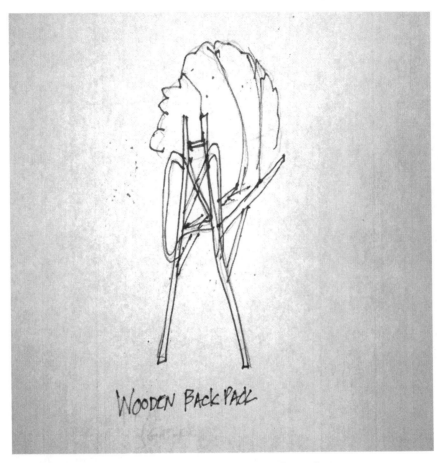

WOODEN BACK PACK

A-frame wooden backpack

Other everyday jobs included sweeping out the buildings with a straw broom, picking up trash, and keeping the whole complex clean. When I think about the struggle parents today have telling their seven-year olds to clean their rooms and keep them clean, it amazes me how little choice I had when these values were instilled in me. If we refused to do our chores, we would get whipped severely with thin sticks. We knew what our place was, and unless we were foolish, we didn't step out from that place.

Unfortunately, I was more on the foolish side when I first came there. I tried to run away from the orphanage several times during the year. I was always caught and dragged back to be whipped in front of everyone as an example of what not to do. You would think after the first couple times I would have learned the lesson, but I was pretty strong-willed. One time I actually made it all the way to a shop in the village and only got caught when I tried to steal some food. The owner dragged me back to the orphanage and that was the last time I decided to try to run away.

* * *

The least desirable job at the orphanage was one that I thankfully never had to do. I was too young at the time to do it, but I can remember vividly watching the other boys who were allotted the task, usually the oldest and strongest of us all. They used a long stick with a large bucket attached at either end. They would carry the empty buckets to the hole in the ground that we used as our toilet, and set it down. They used shovels to load up the human waste into the buckets as full as they could carry. Fuller buckets meant a heavier load, but it also got the job done quicker. They would then carry the buckets to a rice field farther away and empty them there. That was some of the best rice I have ever seen; always growing like there was no tomorrow!

Speaking of tomorrows, that is what my life at that point had become. Every day seemed a repeat of the last, with nothing to look forward to except for the next tomorrow.

* * *

We ate breakfast at sun up every morning and then went to work in the rice field. I finally settled into the permanent job of making breakfast for the entire orphanage. I would get up very early in the morning, well before sunrise, to prepare breakfast for them; at seven years old, I was "the cook." Sometimes if there was not enough wood gathered from the day before, I would have to go up the hill by myself, gather more wood, and then hike down the hill to the dining room to get the fire ready to start the rice. This was my job, and all the kids depended on me to deliver every morning.

Making the rice was pretty simple. All I had to do is get water into the black kettle, and then dump the huge sack of brown rice into the kettle and watch it boil, stir a couple times, and then let it do its thing. The hardest part was dumping the heavy rice bag into the kettle, since I was very small at seven years old. I had to use a long flat piece of wood propped up to lean like a ramp over one side of the kettle. I would slide the bag up and along the length of the piece of wood with all my strength until it reached the kettle. Then I would slice open the bag with a knife and let the rice fall into the pot of cold water. Day after day I did this; that was my routine.

* * *

The first few times I did my job of making rice, I did not do very well. I made many mistakes including mishandling the rice into the kettle so that it spilled everywhere; burning out the fire; or cooking too long and burning the rice; and so on and so on. I even dumped a few kettles onto the ground as I was preparing it and had to start the entire process all over again. I think after about a week I felt better and more comfortable with what I was doing. Before I knew it, I had been doing it for almost two years. I must have been doing okay because no one got sick from eating my food, or maybe they just didn't tell me.

For three meals every day it was pretty simple for us kids: rice, rice, and more rice. It was almost always brown rice, but for a special treat once in a while we would get white rice. Instead of drinking water every day, we would sometimes get powdered milk to mix into our water. These days were few and far between, but we always looked forward to them.

* * *

Sometimes we'd get a little creative and go looking for some meat, such as frogs, snakes and grasshoppers. We would have to hunt them. Hunting was fun. We did it in a group, and we celebrated as a team by sharing our prizes with everyone at the orphanage. I think the actual hunting was better than eating them, but eating them was fun, too. That was one thing we believed in at the orphanage, that there was no competition. We were all in this together, and we depended on each other for everything. Some of the friendships that I developed with the other boys were the truest ones I ever had in my whole life.

The process of catching frogs was an art. First, you had to make the weapon. You needed a thick metal wire, about ¼-inch thick and about twenty-four inches long. We sharpened one end with rocks, either by hammering it down between two rocks to make it flat and sharp, or by rubbing the tip back and forth on a large rock to sharpen it. We then looped the other end around it to make a circle, and then attached a rubber band to it. This was a make-shift sling shot. The rubber band went around the thumb, ran across the palm, and then attached to the pinky finger. With our other hand, we would pull back the loop end toward our bodies like when shooting a bow and arrow. When you spotted your prey, you let go and the metal "arrow" would hopefully hit the target. There you have it, a nice sling arrow weapon to hunt frogs. It was very effective. On a typical day, we would catch seventy to eighty frogs ... not bad for a day's work!

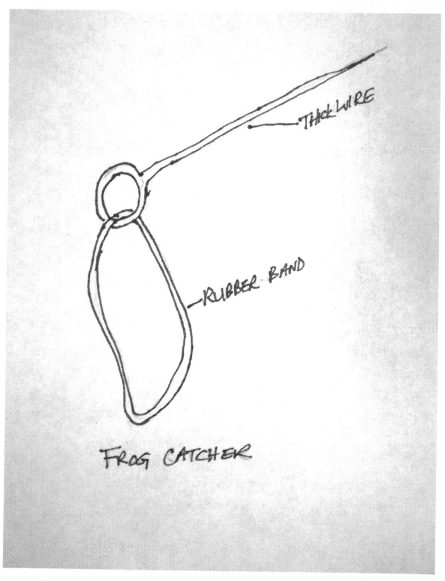

Frog catcher made of thick wire and a rubber band

Our second gourmet food was fried grasshoppers. Basically, we would have a round net with a pole similar to those used to catch butterflies. Once we chased and captured one, we would thread a thin wire through the hard shell at the base of its neck, just like stringing popcorn. We would add more and more as we went along, until eventually we would each have a two-foot long string of bugs. All the boys would combine our catches, and slide them off the wires into a large iron pan. We would toast them over the fire until they turned brown and crispy. We would eat the whole bug, legs, tails, everything; nothing went to waste. When you were only given three bowls of rice a day, bugs and other creatures became a gourmet meal. It gave us the protein we needed to nourish our growing bodies, but at the time, we didn't look at it like that. To us, it was a way to satiate our hunger, and besides, they really did taste good!

Those were our two main sources of meat, but every once in a while a boy was lucky enough to stumble across some unlucky snake who became a tasty treat for us. When I think back now of eating these things, it doesn't appeal to me in the least, but at the time, when that was all we had, and all we knew, it seemed natural enough.

So that was pretty much how we would spend what little spare time we had. We would also read books that they provided for us. The orphanage had people who would teach us how to read and write in Korean. We did not go to a separate school in the village; instead, we just sat on the floor in one of the buildings, or outside during the warmer months, and learned. We had regular paper and used leftover wood ash from the fire as chalk to write. We were not separated by age; rather it was more like a one-room school house, with all of us learning at the same time. Some older kids were more advanced, so they would help out the younger kids.

It wasn't a great life, but at least it was predictable. We had food, clothing and shelter, and knew what was expected of us each day.

Time passed, and no one adopted me.

Chapter 4

Moving On Up

It was now August of 1972 and I had been at Hwa Saeng Won for over three years. I had bonded with these new "brothers" of mine. We depended on each other for survival in a similar way that my biological brothers and I had, and I was now comfortable in the daily routines that we had established. Even though our lives were rough in many ways, there was a comfortable predictability to them. We each had our place in the orphanage; a job, a purpose. We woke one morning to discover that Hwa Saeng Won was closing, and many of us were being transferred to a new orphanage called Holt Children's Services in Seoul. I was now nine years old, and was worried that they could just put me out on the street if I refused to go because I was getting close to the age when I would be unadoptable. So although I was afraid to go to a new orphanage and have to start all over again, I was relieved that I was even going at all.

Holt Orphanage came about through the work started by Americans Harry and Bertha Holt after the Korean War ended in 1953. They lived in Creswell, Oregon, and were touched by the plight of so many children who were fathered by American servicemen during the Korean War. These children were treated as outcasts by their Korean villages due to their mixed heritage. Many were homeless and starving to death through no fault of their own. In 1956, Harry and Bertha ended up adopting eight Korean orphans even though they already had six children of their own. They helped many other orphans around the world find homes in the United States, and soon opened the orphanage that I was now heading to as my new home.

Although at the time I knew nothing about this new place to which I was being sent, I was at least glad that Holt would still take me in. Little did I know just how drastically my life would change because of Holt Orphanage.

* * *

Not only did I have a new home, but at Holt, I also got a new name. I became Kim Jin Soo. Not by any choice or intention of mine, or anyone else's for that matter. Rather, it happened due to a simple mistake. The woman in charge of my intake papers at Holt asked me my name. I told her Kim *Ji* Soo. She wrote down Kim *Jin* Soo as she miscopied it from the information book handed over from Hwa Saeng Won. Everyone at the orphanage from then on called me Jin instead of Ji. I spoke up in the beginning to tell them my name was Ji, not Jin, but after a while it became futile. No one believed me, or simply didn't have the time to deal with it. Just like the start of my life, this, too, was out of my control. I was now Jin Soo, and that was that.

* * *

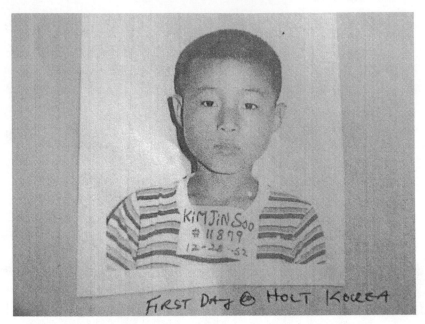

FiRST DAy @ HOLT KOREA

My entrance photo to Holt Orphanage. Boys' hair was kept short at Hwa Saeng Won to try to prevent lice and to eliminate the need for grooming. Holt allowed us to grow our hair longer.

The new orphanage was a whole new world. There were a lot of large buildings there, and we were now able to be separated by age group and gender. It was like going from a budget level motel to a five star hotel. It was bigger, cleaner, and offered so many more opportunities than what I had been accustomed to at Hwa Saeng Won.

The kids already living there were cleaner, too. They were well- dressed and well- groomed compared to how we had been in Hwa Saeng Won. Even though their clothes were still pretty plain and simple, to me they were so much nicer than the clothing I'd been wearing. We were given t-shirts and khaki-colored pants, and several sets of each! We were still responsible for laundering our own clothes, but rather than each boy washing his own clothes, it was done as a group activity. Bigger kids would help the smaller ones like a family network. We still washed them in a creek, but we enjoyed it more now than before, and it was viewed less like a chore because we would sing and laugh together as we enjoyed each other's company. This was a new experience, because in the old orphanage, everyone was afraid to talk during our work; we were afraid that we may get sent somewhere worse, or put out onto the streets.

Holt organized the living areas better than I had experienced at Hwa Saeng Won. We were grouped together by age, with girls and boys separated and put into different buildings. I was placed in the boys' dormitory with thirty-two other boys from eight to twenty-two years of age. Unlike my first orphanage, Holt did not abide by the practice of releasing children to the streets or to the military once they reached a certain age. The boys who were older who did not get adopted became part of Holt by working there so they could still stay.

The rooms were big and clean and had large windows. They also had something I had never known in my whole life: real beds! The bedroom was one big room with beds arranged in long lines up against every wall. They were wooden bunk beds, and even though there was no mattress—just a plank of wood with a layer of canvas placed across it—it was the first time in my life I was actually up off of the floor to sleep. Bunk beds were necessary so that they could fit more of us in there.

The luxuries in this place were unimaginable to me. We were given soap, real toothbrushes and "toothpaste": a fine powdered salt mixture. There was a genuine wooden outhouse outside with a roof on it, rather than the plain hole in the ground we had at the old place.

There were no chores to do like the rice picking, or the "doo-doo dipping and hauling" that we had to do at the old place, but we did have basic responsibilities, like keeping the complex clean every day. We had to sweep each building daily, but we would work together in groups to get it done quickly.

However, what stood out to me as the best, as I would imagine it would to most people in my situation, was the abundance and variety of food! There was more food at one meal than I had ever seen in my whole life! We actually had different types of the authentic foods that Korean people were used to, like kimchee, a delicious, spicy pickled cabbage that was eaten at every meal. Besides rice, it is the one staple food that Korea is known for. Other dishes consisted of meats, fruits and vegetables, with spices of all kinds and flavors. I thought I had died and gone to heaven with all the new tastes and colors that were placed before me at each meal. My intake papers at the orphanage stated that I was "not choosy about foods." Compared to what I had eaten in the past to just stay alive, I had no need to be choosy when I was presented with a complete smorgasbord three times a day!

This was also the first time in my life that I had been formally introduced to religion. We had a church in one of the buildings where we held services. Everyone would gather together there to read the Bible and learn about God and his amazing love and power. We finally felt like human beings because we learned we were all created by God who loved us equally. Rather than having our purpose in life dictated by the jobs we were expected to carry out each day, we now were given the chance to realize that our purpose in life was given from God when He gave us each life. We became Christians, and gave thanks to God for each and every one of us. We learned that God didn't love us any less just because we were orphans. In fact, we felt that sometimes He may even have loved us more.

Chapter 5

Others

I was now ten years old. At least that is what I had always thought. When I arrived at Holt, I told them my birthday was April 2, 1962. However, there were a lot of discrepancies that were made in my records from the old orphanage that Holt could not verify. Holt had my birthdate listed as December 28, 1962, and since there was no way I could prove that it wasn't, that is what stuck. So, I instantly became eight and a half months younger. I am glad now that they did that because I was always afraid of "aging out" before I could get adopted. The older boys who were still there knew that they were there to help out the younger kids. However, it was so unusual for families to want to adopt older children that the chance of them finding a "forever home" and leaving the orphanage was pretty much gone.

Up until this point, I never had contact with any children who weren't in my exact situation. From my biological brothers, to the kids at the first orphanage, and now all of us together at Holt, we all shared one common bond: we were orphans. We bonded with each other and felt like we had found our niche; we never worried about competing with each other, because to each other, we were all the same. We didn't know what it was like to be in any different type of situation other than an orphanage setting. I don't think we were prepared for what came when we met the "others": kids who had real families and homes.

Holt was much more advanced in how we were educated than my past days of learning on the dirt floors of Hwa Saeng Won. We were expected to attend a regular public school. While the schools in Seoul weren't all that fancy, they were still more overwhelming than anything I had ever experienced.

I was placed in the fifth grade at Ilsan Primary School. The school was very structured and there were specific processes and rules that we were expected to follow. The school culture was very strict. You did not speak unless spoken to, and ALWAYS raised your hand before doing so.

Classrooms were small and always packed wall to wall with kids. We had actual desks and chairs, which were all so different for me. I wasn't used to sitting up straight in a hard chair for hours and hours on end.

We started each day with morning stretching exercises in the front yard of the school. Everyone, students and teachers alike, participated. This was to get our minds and bodies fresh and ready to absorb the lessons of the day. We would all spread out, row after row, a sea of children, ready to follow the leader.

The schoolwork was very difficult and intense. The purpose of being there was to learn. There was no fooling around permitted at all, and anyone foolish enough to try would either get beaten with a long skinny stick, or rapped across the open palm of your hand with a piece of wood similar to a ruler. Everyone had to sit up straight all the time. There was no slouching or bending over allowed at any time in the classroom. Even if we were just reading a book, we had to sit up straight with the book in our outstretched arms and our backs as straight as a board.

Homework was a serious task as well. We were expected to always complete our homework, no matter what kind of other responsibilities awaited us at home. For example, at the orphanage, we had chores to do when we got back, like our laundry or sweeping the houses, so sometimes we were too tired afterwards and the homework didn't get done. I was a serious offender when it came to this. I wasn't mature enough yet to manage my time right, and that is what the school was setting out to teach us. I was in a catch-22: I would get in trouble for not having my homework done, and then, after getting a beating from the teacher, have to stay after school to complete it. By the time I got back to the orphanage, I was already behind with my chores. I would have to do them after it was already dark outside, and by the time I was through, I would be too tired again to do my new homework. Then the whole process would repeat itself the next day in my seemingly never-ending cycle of self-defeat.

This didn't mean I wasn't a bright student. I always did well on the work and understood everything; I just didn't know how to do everything I was supposed to do at the time I was supposed to do it. Then one day, one of my "brothers" from the orphanage took pity on me. He was a bit older, and was willing to listen to my struggles. He worked with me each day to figure out how to do my chores in a more efficient time frame so that I could get my homework completed right after. He ended up getting adopted shortly afterward, so I didn't really get time to say thanks to him for helping me to learn one of my now strongest qualities: time management.

* * *

We all walked the couple miles to the school building in a big group. We must have stuck out to the other kids like a sore thumb. Although the clothes we had on were nice in our humble opinion, they must have seemed shabby to the other kids because we were often laughed at and called names. They made fun of us for being homeless and having no parents.

This went on day after day until finally I lost my temper. A boy was riding past our group on his bicycle and calling us names and making faces at us. I kicked his tire as he went past and he fell off of his bike. We got into a fist fight and we both got in some good licks before we gave in and called it even. That was the day I decided that I had better start taking the Tae Kwon Do lessons that were given at the new orphanage. I knew that if my life was not going to get better by way of having a family, then I needed to learn ways to get some sort of control in my life. Tae Kwon Do taught us to relax, manage stress, think peaceful thoughts, and build confidence and character. My school work actually got better as I learned to become more disciplined, and realized that my own mind and body were something that I could have control over.

The classes were held twice a day: early in the morning before school, and after school. I was so fascinated with this new experience of finally having some peace and stability within my grasp that I dedicated myself to learning the art. Within a short period of time, I become a black belt in Tae Kwon Do, and felt more positive about myself than I had since becoming an orphan.

* * *

In November of 1972, a woman came to visit with me. She told the staff that she was my aunt, wife of my father's brother. When I saw her, I did not recognize her at all. She said my uncle, who was supposedly an army colonel, would come to see me, but that never happened. She said she did not know the whereabouts of my parents. I did not know what to make of her so I did not say much. She finally left and never came back. I did not know who she was and no one at the orphanage was careful enough to ask her name, address, or any other identifying details. I told Holt I did not know anything about either an aunt or an uncle. I can only wonder what would have become of me if I had gone with this mysterious stranger.

* * *

Because of the new orphanage, winter actually became an enjoyable time. I was used to always having to fight for warmth and heat when sleeping in a drafty room, or under cornstalks. Winter had always been a cold, desperate time for me. But at Holt, it was much different. The rooms were nicer and warmer, and we had blankets on our beds. Since I was up off the floor, I didn't have to shiver myself to sleep each night.

We actually felt comfortable enough to start playing outside. Since we knew we had a place where we could go inside to warm up, we learned that it was okay to go out and have fun in the cold for a change.

In the bitterest cold, the water-logged rice field would freeze over and make an ideal ice skating rink. We would fashion a pair of "skates" out of a piece of wood and wire to fit the length of our shoe. The wire was wound around the wood and rested along the bottom to form a "blade."

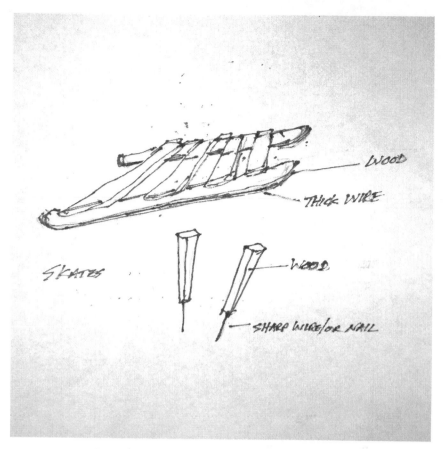

Ice skates made from wood and wire

We tied the skates to our feet, and I couldn't remember when I had ever had so much fun for the sake of having fun. True, it was fun when I was hunting frogs and grasshoppers with my old orphanage-mates in the first orphanage, but that was fun with an underlying purpose. We were hungry, and needed to hunt for extra food. This time was different ... we weren't in need of anything, and we let ourselves go and just enjoyed being carefree.

We also figured out how to make a "sled" out of a large, flat piece of wood with two smaller pieces of wood attached underneath with a wire for runners.   This was for the younger kids who didn't know how to skate. They would take a long wooden stick that had been sharpened to a point on one end, and push themselves along the ice as they sat on the sled, much like a skier would use poles to propel himself along.

Those were our fun times. We didn't have any toys, so we were elated when we had something to play with in what little spare time we had around school, chores and other responsibilities. We finally got to play like regular children, and it felt great.

We often had visitors come to see us. They were GI's from America, and they would sing songs to us in English and give us candy. The only two songs I remembered were "Oh Susannah" and "You Are My Sunshine." I sang those all the time when I was doing my chores or walking to school. Little did I know at the time that for me it was just the beginning of learning English.

Chapter 6

Letters from Heaven

Part of life in an orphanage is hoping that someday you may get adopted by a family who wants to keep you as their own. You are always wishing every day that it will be your day, your turn for a warm home and a loving family. You learn early in an orphanage that life isn't fair; it is the main reason you are even there. However, for the older kids or kids with special needs, you also knew your chances of "getting out" were not the best. People simply didn't want older kids, even if we were perfectly healthy. We were too often considered by potential parents outside of Korea to have too many "cultural and social issues" to make the adjustment to be a member of their family.

By now I was ten years old. I had just spent the last four years of my childhood as an orphan, and was in my second orphanage. Although life was much better here, the fact that I was an orphan never escaped me. I longed for a home of my own, with people who would love and care for me, and want me in their lives forever. I missed Kyang Soo and Yae Soo terribly, and buried any thoughts of them deep in my mind to help numb the incredible pain.

When families wanted to adopt, everyone chose the younger children and the babies. I can't tell you how many times I watched a baby come in and go out before me. The babies had it the easiest, because they didn't even understand their situation. They didn't know they were in an orphanage, like we older kids understood all too well.

* * *

There was a certain process that was followed when one of us was going to get adopted. A child would get a letter from the orphanage saying that it was a notice that someone in America wanted to adopt him or her. The staff would show us a picture of the parents, along with a letter from them. It was written in English, and translated for us into Korean.

Every day we hoped to be the one to get a letter. It was what we thought about when we first woke up in the morning, and the last thing we thought about before we went to sleep at night. We prayed all the time, and it was always in the forefront of our minds. Nothing we did was more important than getting that letter saying that we would finally be given a home.

Like I mentioned earlier, most of the kids who got the letters were there the shortest time. I saw a lot of my friends who were much younger get letters, pack up their few belongings, and leave. While I was happy for them, on the inside I would die a little more each time. I knew that the older you got in the orphanage, the lower the chances that someone would adopt you. I just kept hoping and praying that I would get my letter someday soon.

So, day after day of watching other kids around me get letters, I got more and more discouraged. I wondered what would become of me. I knew I was a good kid; I obeyed the adults, did my chores, worked hard, got good grades, and got along well with everyone. But age was creeping up slowly, and constantly reminding me that this could be my forever home.

38

But a bigger miracle was just around the corner, and if miracles are one per customer, I got more than my share that year.

What I had been waiting for had finally happened. It was spring of 1973. I was ten years old, and I got a letter.

Chapter 7

Coming to America

I cried. Not just a little, but for days and days. I was happy. I was scared. I was overjoyed. I was frightened. All of these feelings washed over me like a great tidal wave of emotions. Happy because my wish had come true, but scared because of what my future may hold. I was going to America, and I was overwhelmed. I never thought too much about it because I was too old to think that it could become a reality. Once I turned ten, I pretty much gave up and had resigned myself to growing up in Holt or wherever they wanted to put me. In all the time I had been in both orphanages, I had never again heard from my biological parents or my brothers. I just figured at this point, they must have no longer wanted me either.

The thought of a new Mom and Dad, in our own house in America, really didn't sink in.

Their names were Frank and Patricia Stearns, and they lived in Greenville, Pennsylvania. They were both elementary school teachers and had no children of their own. They were interested in adopting an older child, and since I was the first one they saw in a booklet sent to them by Holt, they said they would take me or one just like me. Luckily for all of us I was not exactly in high demand, so it was an easy match to make.

Even though I read their words, and understood them, I still had reservations in the back of my mind: they could change their minds and call the whole thing off. So while I was happy, I was also cautious not to get too attached to them because it could all be over with another letter.

* * *

I wrote back to them several times, and my words, carefully crafted by my own hand in Korean, were translated into English so that we could communicate:

April, 1973

11879   KIM JIN SOO
HOLT CHILDREN'S HOME

Dearest my parents

What's new ?

I got your lovely picture and good news with great pleasure and especially
the good news makes me so very happy. I can not put into words how
happy I was when I heard it first.

I am quite doing well in the love of our Savior Jesus Christ
who died for our sin and will come again in the near future and I am
studying very hard. And gets along well with other children as I playing
foot-ball, base-ball and the other sports.

Often, I think, I will be a best loved boy in our new home
for there is no child except *me*. And My new mom and dad will love me so
very much when I got there. And thanks to God that He prepares a good
home, mom and dad who will loves me all the time.

I am sending you my love and kiss and I want to say good bye
from here. May God's blessing on you and your job all through the
year.

Your loved son

Kim Jin Soo

Sin 4-11-73

This is the first letter I wrote to my new parents, Frank and
Patricia Stearns. Since it was written by me first in Korean,
and then translated and typed by someone else into
English, the wording is a little awkward!

April, 1973

My dear mom & dad

How is everything going on around you in the grace of Our Savior Jesus Christ ? Your letter made me so very happy and no words are glad enough to express my mind as I get it.

Mom and dad, I like to ride cycle very much and sometimes, we used to enjoys it in our ground. I am learning now Korean language, mathematics, history, and the kind but I have a genius for language and mathematics. And I am very happy that dad is a teacher.

I love most of the sports but especially, I like football and baseball. I can ride cycle well. I love yellow color so that I think it's better to paint yellow color for my room. You sounded me that you show my picture to many people and I show your photograph to our roommates and other people. They used to say, your house looks like very good and your new mom and dad seems like very kind people. I am very anxious to see you sooner or later.

Please pray together that I could go to your side soon. well I will end it for now and may God be with you all the time. Good bye...

Your love son

Jin Soo

Sn&5-23-73

This is the second letter I sent to my adoptive parents. Even though the translation is imperfect, it is pretty clear I was excited about my new family and home!

My dear parents

I want to say hello to all of you in the grace of our Savior Jesus Christ? I am quite doing well due to your love, pray and continuial supporting.

I got your lovely letter with great pleasure. I can not put into words how happy I was when I received it. My interesting subject is painting. We had good Easter morning services.

I am getting along pretty well in the love of our Lord God who gave me new life and take care of us. I am healthy. I believe all of the things are done bye our Savior Jesus Christ who goes with us always.

There are some boys who aged same with me, they were so glad and makes me so very happy when they heard that I could go to my new family in the near day. Maybe, there will be a big events when I go to your home. I am very anxious to see you sooner or later.

I am riding cycle and some boys afe learning it. I am a good cycle boy. And I used to plays with other children as we playing ball, cycling and the kind on each other with joy.

I'll end it for now and may God bless you richly all the time. Would you pray for me that I could go to you home sooner or later as your new son. Good bye........................

Truely your son
Kim Jin Soo

Sung 6-14 73

This is the third letter I sent to my new parents.

While I was happy to be leaving, I had to leave many good friends behind. I did not have much to pack except for a couple personal items: my Tae Kwon Do uniform, a set of clothes, a Korean bible, and pictures of my new parents, Frank and Pat Stearns. I also took along the letters that they had written to me. I did not take anything to remember Holt because they really didn't have anything back then. It was mainly just me and my body and the few personal items I carried with me in a small carry-on bag. It didn't bother me that I didn't have much to take. Truthfully, at that point I would have been happy to go there butt-naked as long as I could get a real family and home. I was on such an adrenaline rush of happiness and excitement to be finally leaving that I couldn't really think about much else.

It did not fully sink in that I was going to America to live with my new family until I boarded the plane headed to New York City. I knew then that it was for real. I was going to have a real home.

Chapter 8

Land of the Free

I still could not escape the responsibilities of the orphanage. In 1973, families did not come to Korea to get their adopted child. Instead, the children were all boarded onto an airplane and flown over as one big group to meet our new parents at the airport gate. Since I was the oldest child, I had the responsibility of taking care of all the babies and little ones riding on the plane with me. The flight attendants were busy doing other duties so they were grateful to have me assist with changings, feedings, and comforting the babies on the long seventeen-hour flight. I was grateful to keep busy so I didn't have to think too much or have time to be afraid.

I did not know anything about the people who were adopting me except for their names, what they looked like in a small color photo, and the brief words we had exchanged in the few letters that had been through multiple translations. They looked kind and gentle from their picture, and their words gave me comfort that they must really want me to be their son, or else why would they invite me to live with them halfway across the world? So many thoughts raced through my mind, but I didn't have it in me any more to be scared. I had been through so much upheaval and uncertainty in my young life that I knew I could adapt to whatever lay ahead, for better or for worse.

When the plane touched down in New York City, I felt a flutter of different emotions. How would this new family like me? What if they wanted to send me back? What if I did not like them and I wanted to go back? Would they let me back onto the plane? What would they think of how I looked? I was wearing white shorts, a blue-green button-up shirt, and white socks with tennis shoes. I certainly felt like a million bucks as these were the nicest clothes I had ever owned in my entire life.

As the stewardess started helping me gather my belongings (which were now contained inside a small white backpack given to me on the plane), it was too late to do anything except take a deep breath and ready myself to meet my new family.

Our meeting each other for the first time was a strange set-up. I had only the small photograph of my new parents to guide me through the throngs of people at the gate, searching faces to find the couple that matched the one in my photo. My new parents had to do the same. They had two black and white photos of me, one taken when I was first transferred over to Holt, and the other taken eleven months later when I was discharged from Holt for good.

I think it was easier for them to find me because I stood out in a crowd with my dark Asian hair and eyes. All the people I saw in the airport looked so much alike to me. Most of them had light colored faces, but hair colors of all types. It was confusing to try to take it all in. I would see someone with brown hair like in my new mother's picture, but I could not be sure it was her because there were so many other people there with brown hair. I did not have much experience looking at big groups of American people all in one place. This was going to be difficult.

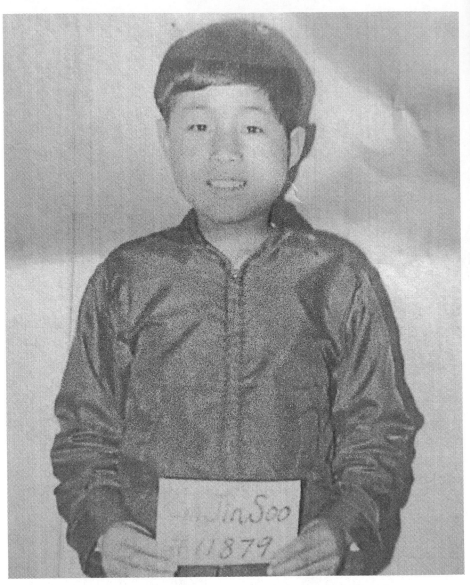

This is the last photo taken of me as I left Holt Orphanage to come to America. You can see from the differences in this photo and the one they took on my first day there that I looked healthier and happier because of their care.

I used a photo of my parents to try to identify them for the first time at the airport.

Luckily, it was them who spotted me and waved enthusiastically. We finally found each other and confirmed a match. I just smiled. I could not speak any English and they could not speak any Korean, so we just looked at each other and smiled. Then they both leaned in and embraced me in a group hug so natural that I knew this is where I belonged. They say that a smile is understood in any language, and that is all we needed. I knew these were good people, and I relaxed and let them hug me, and hugged them back.

They let go of me only long enough to sign the paperwork needed to finalize my arrival into their custody, and then we were off, hand in hand, like a real family, to catch another flight back to Pittsburgh, Pennsylvania. This was the true beginning of my life. Up until now, I felt like I had just merely existed. Now I finally belonged. This was real. This was *home*.

Chapter 9

Greenville, PA July 1973

The plane ride to Pittsburgh was a quiet one due to our language barriers. Then came the car ride back to Greenville, another hour and a half to my new home. I had never ridden in a car before. In Korea, when we traveled at the orphanage, it was either by walking or by riding in a small cart pulled by cows. By the time we reached Greenville, I was quite carsick. Mom gave me a little Coca-Cola to drink to settle my stomach, but I had never had anything like that before. To me it tasted like poison. I started to wonder what I was getting myself into in this strange new land. It was my first night and I already thought they were trying to kill me with this dirty water.

* * *

Mom and Dad had never been able to have children of their own, but knew that they always wanted to be parents. They were schoolteachers; Mom taught second grade, and dad taught third. Their kindness and love for children was enormous, and they soon turned to adoption to make their dreams of parenthood come true. They looked into many avenues, from domestic to foreign adoptions, and were overwhelmed with all the information presented to them. They had been in the process of looking at several situations at the same time, and if not for the grace of God, I may not have been with them at all.

One place they were looking into at the same time as Holt International was a local Pennsylvania agency that had a baby girl up for adoption. Since Mom and Dad had already submitted paperwork to be considered as adoptive parents at Holt, this other agency was reluctant to let them take the baby. I guess there was a rule that you could not be working on more than one adoption at a time.

When they got a call, several days before Holt contacted them to let them know if I was even still available, it could have been the end of the road for me. The local adoption agency had the baby and decided that Mom and Dad needed to take her that day. If they could not, they would place her with someone else. Mom and Dad thought about it and told the agency to go ahead and place her with someone else. They had invested a lot of time in communicating back and forth with Holt, and were not quite ready to just leave the situation hanging. That is what made me realize that I must have been hand-picked by God to be with Frank and Pat Stearns, because with one little word to the other agency, my dream of a family would have been shattered.

It still amazes me how they ended up choosing me. They had been only looking at younger kids, like most people usually do, when they were sent a brochure from Holt International in South Korea. In it was a section on kids who were ten years and older who still needed to find homes. They skimmed through all the information, but there was only one picture on the page. It was me. I was a bright, wide-eyed ten-year-old who had been orphaned and needed a loving family to complete my life. Mom said that there was something about the picture of me and the paragraph about the older kids that changed their views that day. When people asked them later why they decided on an older child, she explained that if two elementary school teachers weren't capable of handling a ten-year-old boy, then not many people were! She wrote a letter to Holt the very next day requesting to adopt me or a similar child if I was no longer available. She later told me that there was just something in her faith that she could not shake that day. They just knew I was the one.

* * *

July 11, 1973 was my first full day in America. I was introduced to even more family. It was amazing to me. I not only had parents now, but I also had an Aunt Sandi (Mom's sister) and two Grandmas and two Grandpas! I was one lucky fellow. Although Mom and Dad tried to keep visitors outside the family to a minimum, I learned I was one hot commodity. Friends and neighbors from all around town dropped in to meet the new addition to the family. Since I could not speak any English, I just sat and stared at everyone until they left. My parents probably wondered what they had gotten themselves into. They had attempted to learn a few Korean words like *Grandma*, *Grandpa*, *bathroom*, and *good night*, but their pronunciation was awful. The only words I didn't mind hearing all mangled up were "I love you." I was not in any hurry to learn English until the moment when I realized it was necessary for my survival.

We lived in a big white house on York Street. I was all wound up from the excitement of meeting people and taking in all the many rooms of this beautiful new place. My entire first house in Korea would have fit inside just one of the rooms in this new home! Then I realized I needed to use the bathroom. I went out the back door and looked for the "hole" I was used to using in Korea. There was none.

I thought maybe the small garage was a gigantic outhouse, but no luck. There was only a car and some tools inside. By this time, I really needed to pee and was getting more and more frustrated. I didn't want to insult my new family by peeing in their yard so I ran back inside and bounced around. My parents, from their experience as schoolteachers, seemed to know what the problem was. My dad led me up the stairs and opened a door to a grand room. There were shiny white porcelain objects all around. It was very confusing. I wasn't sure why I was there.

Dad finally figured out I did not know anything about sinks, toilets or tubs. He took a cup of water from the sink and poured it down the toilet and flushed. I then understood what I was supposed to do. He turned around and stepped aside and I relieved myself in the toilet, although the tub would have made a better target. When I was finished, I discovered the wonders of flushing. I flushed the toilet. Then again. And again. And again. It was fascinating to behold. Where did that water come from? Where did it go? Then an awful thought struck me! Mom was downstairs! I had flushed the toilet, and the water was going downstairs where Mom was sitting! If it fell on her, would they send me back? I raced down the stairs, and to my relief she was safe and dry. I later secretly followed all the pipes around the house until I learned that the waste magically left the house through a pipe in the basement. I would never have to do doo-doo dipping in America!

* * *

54

English as a Second Language (ESL) experts call the time frame when I first came here as a "honeymoon period." This is because everything is bright and shiny and exciting to experience, and like a couple on their honeymoon, everything is wonderful.

I was excited to discover each new object, and observe how people here acted and talked. It was so different from the world I had known, which now seemed so far away. Even simple things like dandelions were fascinating; they would start out as a beautiful yellow flower and quickly turn into a majestic white puffball that could carry away wishes in a single breath. I had no more wishes at this point, because now that I had a real family and a secure home, all my wishes had come true. Even the allergies I was developing after being exposed to all the flora in my new environment couldn't dampen my enthusiasm.

In those first few weeks, I was like a little sponge. I absorbed every word and imitated the actions of everyone I met. I couldn't wait to fit in. I practiced saying basic words and phrases in English, and listened to every word around me, and although I missed being able to talk to anyone or understand what was being said around me, it was a happy time. I wanted to learn English so badly because I had so much I wanted to say to this wonderful family who had given me a chance.

* * *

However, ESL experts also recognize something important about the "honeymoon period" for newcomers to the English language: The period doesn't last long. After all the excitement and delirium of experiencing "firsts" and "news" in my amazing new country, I soon hit a wall. I realized after a few weeks of trying to learn everything I could about this amazing new place that it was HARD. Everyone looked, behaved and talked so much differently than I ever had imagined. I did not know how to communicate beyond gestures and pointing. I know I must have appeared stupid to everyone who was around me. I couldn't even ask for simple things in words, like a drink. It was so frustrating because I knew I wasn't stupid. I had come through so much in Korea, and had been told there I was very bright and mature for my age. Here I could communicate no better than a baby.

It was also difficult for me to figure out the differences with the day and night due to the time zone changes. I was tired during the day and wound up at night. I felt so lost in this new place. At the orphanage, at least I could communicate. My frustration grew and grew until one night it boiled over.

Around nine o'clock one night, Dad told me through his newly learned charades that it was bedtime for me. I was not tired, and my watch did not agree. I was still on Korean time and wanted to explore the house. Dad patiently insisted, but my frustrations grew. I raced up the stairs and grabbed my white backpack from the airplane. I was resorting to the only solution I knew when I was faced with an unpleasant situation: I would simply run away. Only this time it was much different than my attempts to run away in Korea. I didn't know where I was, or anything about the neighborhood around me. In Korea, there was a lot of country so it was much easier to disappear until you got hungry. I could communicate with anyone in Korea because we spoke the same language. Here I was at the mercy of pantomiming my needs and did not cope with it very well.

Then there was the problem of being on the second floor. I figured the only way out without being seen was through the window. I opened the window wide enough to squeeze through and looked down. It sure was a long way down, but I wasn't thinking straight. It was a good thing that at that moment Dad and Mom came up to check out what was happening, maybe because they heard the window opening. They were alarmed to see me with one leg out the window and quickly grabbed me by the back of the shirt to pull me back in. I was upset and crying and raving like a madman in Korean, none of which they could understand. They didn't know what to do so Dad held me in a bear hug while Mom ran downstairs to call the doctor. He prescribed a pill for me to relax and calm me down.

After they had given me the pill, I was still restless as we all waited for it to take effect. I was still sitting by the bedroom window. My dad, sitting on the floor by the door on the other side of the room, took a flashlight and rolled it to me across the floor. He had one of his own, and began to flash it on and off to make patterns on the wall adjacent to us. I soon caught on and mimicked his patterns, following along with this new communication game. I even made a few patterns of my own for him to follow. In that brief moment, I knew that these people were willing to do anything to make me feel comfortable. They truly did care about me, and I was making things hard for them. I soon became drowsier and drowsier and eventually drifted off to sleep. My dad must have lifted me up into bed because that is where I awoke a solid twenty-two hours later, refreshed, calmed, and determined to adjust to this new environment quickly so that I could make my new family proud of me.

I never tried to run away from them again.

Chapter 10

Turbulence

The next night I was sitting on the floor in the living room playing cards with my grandma and grandpa. It was a simple card game where each player threw down one card and whoever had the highest was the winner so there was no need for much talking. Out of nowhere I started singing "You Are My Sunshine" in English, a song I had learned from the American GIs at Holt. It was one of the only things I could say well in English. I must have shocked everyone with this perfect English because everyone started laughing and chattering to each other. I could tell it made them happy, so I was even more determined to learn English.

* * *

The one thing that helped me the most was watching the TV show M*A*S*H. The scene was set in South Korea, so I had a familiar setting to comfort me. Sometimes there would be Koreans speaking Korean and I knew what they were saying. The more I watched the show, the more I picked up the patterns and intonations of the English language. I began to put actions and words together, and little by little things started to make sense.

There were several kids in the neighborhood that were around my age. They were very nice and welcomed me. One girl, named Janelle, had particular patience in helping me to adjust. I followed her around like a puppy, and she didn't seem to mind. She took me under her wing and became like a sister to me.

During the next several months, I soon had a group of twelve neighborhood kids whom I called my friends. They never teased me for how different I looked or talked, and gradually I learned how to speak basic English words so that I could converse with them and their parents. They became a huge part of my new life in America, and I don't think I would have adjusted so well without their continuous friendship and support. I spent the whole summer hanging out with them and learning how to be "American."

One afternoon in late summer, Janelle and I walked to a nearby store to buy some snacks. Later, we went back to my house and sat on the front porch to relax. Mom came out to see what we bought. We were eating something that looked like little silver pellets. She took the package from us and found that it was for cake decorating only. She was scared to death we were eating something that would hurt us so she called the doctor right away. He brushed off her concerns by stating, "Humph! New mother! How much silver do you think anyone would waste in a cake decoration? He'll be fine." At least I knew she cared!

After that, mom and I developed an odd sort of unexplainable ESP. I always seemed to sense when she wanted me. She would only have to go out on the front porch and think "It's time to come home now, Jin," and within a few seconds I would be racing down the street calling, "Did you want me, Mom?" It was the strangest thing, but it showed how deep a connection I had with this wonderful woman whom I was now blessed enough to call my mother.

I also had a fascination with cars. They were so exciting to me since I had been used to only walking or riding in carts pulled by cows. I was having so much fun riding in the car one summer afternoon with my Aunt Sandi that I leaned over and honked the horn. Sandi laughed and said something that I didn't understand, so I did it again. She said something again, but this time did not laugh so I did it several more times to try to get her to laugh again. By this time we had caught the attention of a passing police car that put his siren on and pulled us over to see what the matter was. Sandi sheepishly explained to the officer that I was new to cars and he tried to keep a straight face as he warned me not to do it again. I wondered why he was smiling, but now Aunt Sandi was not. This place was going to take a lot of getting used to!

My parents were so proud to have me as a son that they sent out this "birth" announcement:

"Birth Announcement" Letter

Eight York Street
Greenville, Penna.
August 5, 1973

Hello to all,

We Stearns's just want to tell you of our increase in family.
Our son arrived on July 10th at Kennedy Airport in New York.
As you will see he is a little larger and heavier than most
new arrivals, but we are happy with with him just as he is.

Vital statistics:
Name: Jin Soo Stearns
Height: 55 3/4 inches
Weight: 69½ pounds
Birthdate: December 28, 1962
Birthplace: Seoul, Korea
Disposition: Good (most of the time)
Appetite: Too good for today's prices!

Our son is really a terrific boy who shows interest in art and
music and every sport. His popularity with the neighborhood
boys may wane because he usually beats them at such things as
croquet, badminton, volleyball and kickball (he's really trying
to teach them a version of soccer). He has repeatedly skunked his
Dad at checkers, and his pride and joy is his new bicycle.

Jin Soo is good in math and is beginning to pick up some English
words, thanks largely to the kids living nearby. We hope that
by the time school starts he will be speaking well enough to
start in grade 4.

Each day brings a deepening sense of security with his new home
and friends and parents to Jin Soo, and each day brings his
parents to a firmer conviction that this boy was meant to be our
son. We wish to share our joy via this somewhat lengthy
announcement, and to extend our best wishes to you and your
families.

Frank, Pat and Jin Soo Stearns

*You can tell from this letter how much pride my parents
had in me right from the start!*

61

However, summer was coming to a close, and a new school year was about to begin. I did not know what to expect at American schools. I was starting to pick up the language more and more, but still did not know nearly as much as my friends, and often struggled sometimes to get the meaning of what was being said. In Korea, I had just finished fourth grade. I learned that my new American school wanted to place me back in the fourth grade until I learned more English.

Thank God for the determination of my mother. She wanted no part of placing me back. She knew that I was bright and hardworking, and never doubted that I would work hard to close the language gap due to my strong drive to succeed. She insisted that I be placed in the fifth grade with peers of my own age, and she was absolutely right. With the patience of my new fifth grade teacher, and emotional support from my parents and friends, I excelled. Mom even insisted I be placed with the higher-level reading groups because she did not want me to be limited by a less challenging curriculum. She knew I had strong reading and writing skills in my native language, and that this would help me transition into reading and writing in English with more success. She had more faith in me than anyone I had ever met in my life and that made me all the more determined not to disappoint her.

My parents tried hard that first year to protect me from everything. I guess they figured I had been through enough hardship in my life that they did not want me to ever have to experience any more. However, no parent can be around you 24/7, so they could not defend me against the kids at school who did not take too well to people who looked and sounded like me.

I thought that in Korea, it was bad when the kids from school who had families teased us orphans for not having families. By now, I was getting along with the neighborhood kids and their families all summer, and naively assumed all the kids at school would be just as easygoing and friendly. I thought my days of competing with others to fit in were in the past. I thought I had left the concept of being "different" behind when I finally got a family of my own to love and care for me.

I thought wrong.

Chapter 11

Keeping Up with the Joneses ... in Overdrive

There were some kids at school who were just not content to have a kid in their school who looked different and spoke such very broken English. They were good at making fun of me when no one was looking. They would stretch their eyes in a slant with their fingers and look at me and laugh, making fun of the way my eyes were not rounded like theirs. They would talk in a choppy Chinese accent, acting like they were speaking Korean to me. They would call me names in English that I had yet to understand, but could all too well surmise weren't polite things to call someone. One kid told me to "Get back on my boat and go home." I didn't understand what he meant; I didn't come here on a boat, I came here in an airplane. Didn't he know that? Who was the dummy then, me or him? These were all part of my frustration to fit in. I did not know how to speak well enough to verbalize my thoughts, yet I wanted so badly to prove to these kids that I was just the same as them on the inside. Then an idea struck me, and it redefined me in their eyes.

Since I was not good at verbalizing how I was the same, I knew that I could show them in actions. Therefore, I joined every sport that was offered. I was always physically fit, and my years of laboring at tasks in the orphanage had helped me to develop both fine and gross motor skills. I played baseball and basketball, and I played to win. I threw everything I had into being the best. I was determined that

I could play just as good as these American kids, and to my surprise, it soon became known that I was better. I hit home runs and made baskets at a pace unmatched by my schoolmates. Soon, I became the one that everyone wanted on their team. All the pent-up energy I had from not being able to communicate in words was unleashed on the playing field, and I was a force to be reckoned with. To me, it came as easily and as naturally as breathing, and I wondered if it was my strict and survivalist upbringing that had allowed me to have the discipline to become the best. All I knew was that it was my ticket to equality in the eyes of my unconvinced peers. Kids who teased me before finally decided that I was "okay," and maybe "not so bad." The teasing lessened, I made more and more friends, and I decided, after months of trying to adapt to my new surroundings, that life was good.

Chapter 12

Settling In

Fall was exciting because I got to experience my first Halloween ever. I had no concept of this event in Korea. I didn't quite understand the whole premise, but the outcome was a lot of free candy, so I was all for it. I dressed up like Uncle Sam, wearing the colors of my wonderful new country. This costume was my choice, and I thought it was a fitting tribute to the country that had given me a new perspective of life. I think my parents found it a bit odd, but nonetheless, they helped me get it ready and took me out in the neighborhood to show me off.

What a great feeling it was to go "begging" for candy and knowing deep down that I was doing it for enjoyment, not survival like I had so many times in the past.

I also had a strange obsession with a medium-sized tree branch that I had found out in the yard that fall. I insisted to Mom that I be allowed to take it inside and decorate it with Halloween ornaments. Mom humored me and put it in the window like a Christmas tree. When Halloween was over, she was going to throw it out, but I cried and she just kept it in the house for me. It wasn't any special branch or anything. Really, it was kind of ugly, but to me, it was being able to save something and keep it around. I felt that as long as that branch was here through each season, maybe I would be, too. Mom helped me to decorate it at Thanksgiving and Christmas, too.

I had been here for six months by now. Christmas in America was a new experience for me. We celebrated Christmas while I was at Holt by exchanging a small gift we were given from Holt with all the other kids, so by the end of the day, we were able to play with more than thirty different toys when we all shared our gifts with the group.

Mom and Dad wanted me to have the best experience that first Christmas. They got a real tree for us to decorate, but when Christmas was over, I was so upset. I didn't want them to throw away or burn the tree. I just didn't like the idea of them killing the tree. So from then on, for the next several years, they would buy one tree that was cut and another to plant. We would go and plant that tree in the yard so that it could continue its life, and I would always have a living reminder of the strength and beauty that was now always present in my life. To this day, there are 25-foot pine trees growing in the yard at our old house, thanks to me and my insistence on preserving their lives!

For my first Christmas in America, my parents tried to get me almost anything that I picked out of the catalog. One thing I saw was a large battleship toy (about eighteen inches long) that really floated. I ended up getting it, but really had no place to play with it. Come spring, there was a period of frequent and heavy rainstorms that pummeled our area. Most of the homes in the neighborhood had water in their basements, including ours. The firemen were going around the neighborhood trying to pump water out of people's basements. When they came to our house, I followed them downstairs to see what they would do. Mom and Dad came down a little later to see how the firemen were getting along, and there they saw this big fireman and me floating my battleship boat back and forth quietly between us.

Dad was very involved in music. He was a second-grade teacher, but his real passion was music. He was music director at our local church in Greenville, and conducted the Messiah every year at another church. He lived and breathed music and played the organ, piano, trombone, recorder, viola, and pretty much anything musical! I was the only kid at my school whose Mom came to all the sporting events and whose Dad came to all music recitals.

Therefore, it was only a matter of time before I was encouraged to take up an instrument. I chose the trumpet. Determined to be the best at whatever I did, it was not very long before I became good at it. Dad would arrange some hymns for me to play on my trumpet, him on his trombone, and mom on her flute. We would go down in the basement on Sunday nights and practice our hearts out. We didn't know that we were even noticed until one day a neighbor lady asked my mom if she ever hears the Salvation Army band that comes down in our neighborhood on Sunday nights. She just laughed. She was too embarrassed to tell her it was just us!

I taught myself to play "Happy Birthday" so that on January 5, I could play it for Aunt Sandi's birthday. She was so touched that she cried. The social worker who was making the rounds that January to discuss my adjustment to the adoption had no doubts afterwards that I was right where I belonged.

Chapter 13

Home

Two and a half years later, my transition to my new family and country was complete. I felt like this was what I had been searching for my whole life. We were far from rich, but I had come from such poor surroundings that everything my parents provided to me seemed to be fit for a king. I wondered how I had gotten so lucky to have been chosen by this amazing, generous, loving couple whom I proudly called my parents.

My parents had so much joy raising me that they decided to surprise me with some exciting news. They wanted to adopt another boy so I would have a brother to grow up with. By then, I had lost touch with the boys I had grown up with in Holt, so I did not know if any of them were still available for adoption. Mom and Dad had already been looking through more brochures from Holt, and they shared their thoughts with me.

Once they showed me the picture of a little six-year-old boy named David, I knew instantly he was meant to be part of our family. I was excited to have someone in the house who looked more like me, and whom I could show the ropes. Any life I could help change from that of an orphan to one with hope and love via this amazing family was all right in my book.

It wasn't long before we were on our way to New York City to pick up David at the same airport where I had arrived what seemed like a lifetime ago. David was very small and shy, and looked frightened to go with these strange looking people. I stepped up beside them, and David must have seen something comforting in my face because he finally let go of the stewardess' hand and took mine. I knew all too well the thoughts that must have been going through his mind, and I was determined to be the best big brother I could to him.

* * *

Even though we had an extra bedroom, Mom and Dad thought if we shared a room we would get to know each other faster and this would help David to adjust better. They had bought bunk beds for us, and I took the top bunk. But that night, David would not go to bed. Mom put a blanket on the floor and he would fall asleep next to her at night. After a couple of days of this, it finally hit me. I had been so familiar with my American life that I didn't realize what David's experiences had been. Of course he had never slept in a real bed! He was also probably scared that I would fall on him from above in the top bunk.

That day Mom and I disassembled the top bunk and placed the bed onto the floor at the same level as the bottom bed so that they were now side by side. When I went to sleep in my bed that night, David finally slept in his new bed beside me. It was then that I really realized how far I had come in such a short time.

I was having difficulty remembering how to speak Korean because English was now my primary language. I read, wrote, listened and spoke entirely in English now. I never spoke Korean again after I left Korea because I never had a need to. My new environment at home and school were all in English, so I quickly replaced one language with another. I know now that language is a liquid intelligence in the way that the brain stores it, so the adage "Use it or lose it" is completely true if one wants to retain the ability to speak a language.

Chapter 14

The Future Is Bright

David and I got along well, although we had extremely different personalities. I was very headstrong and outgoing, while David was quiet and reserved. I loved sports and being active; he was into books and music. It must have been hard for him to grow up with me always being an overachiever. However, Mom and Dad always loved us both equally, and treasured us for the different joys we brought to the house.

When David went to middle school, a lot of the kids assumed that since he was my little brother, he would excel at sports the same way that I did. This really wasn't fair to him because that wasn't where his interests were, and we were two completely different people. David found his way of "fitting in" to his new world by being more thoughtful and patient, and would just wait to be accepted. I, on the other hand, felt like I always had to fight to prove my worth to earn the respect of others. David did it the easy way. He didn't change for anybody; he just let everyone come around to him in their own time. I had to admire that strategy and wished I had thought of it!

Mom and Dad gave us a good childhood, one that neither of us would have gotten growing up in an orphanage. When I entered high school, I was pretty popular by then. I had found a solid group of friends and was on my way to really knowing who I was. I felt like I had been an American all my life because I had adapted so well to the language and culture. Being Korean was getting more and more distant in my memory.

I went out for football, basketball, and track. I lettered in all of these sports, and played trumpet in both the marching band and jazz band. Jazz band had about fourteen members, and we played opposite nights when there were no football games. My parents came to every one of my games, all sports, all weather; no matter what, they never missed a one. I had good friends, a good family, and a good home life. If you would have asked me eight years earlier if I had ever thought my life would be this great, I would have told you that I could not ever imagine it. In fact, I would have told you that I was never going to live anything beyond the orphanage life which I had grown so accustomed.

I eventually graduated from Greenville High School in 1981. I had been in America for the past nine years, and knew this was where I planned to stay. My family and I had already discussed my future, and I knew I wanted nothing more than to stay in America and continue on to college. I had been dabbling at painting and drawing in some free time and realized I had a natural ability for art. I wanted to go to school to major in art, and then eventually go on to medical school so that I could do anatomical drawings for medical books and other educational literature.

Whatever I decided to do with my life, I knew it was only possible because of the love of my adoptive parents. Frank and Patricia Stearns had taken a wild chance on a little boy nine years earlier about whom they had known nothing except for a name and an age. I was a world away immersed in a culture and language unfamiliar to them, but that didn't dissuade them. They followed their hearts and faith, and entered into so many unknowns as first time parents of a ten-year-old Korean orphan. Because of their strength and love, they provided me with the missing piece that I had always lacked so far in my young life. I gained the confidence to blossom into a well-adjusted human being. While Mom will argue that I have always been a self-made man, I cannot agree with her on this one. Because of the love of two strangers, the linking of our lives together by Holt International, and the strength of a family to weather through any storm, I am who I am today.

It would be almost forty years from the day I set foot in America before I returned to Korea to learn about my past.

Chapter 15

Winning

Some of the best days of my life happened after I graduated from Greenville High School in 1981. I went to college at Indiana University of Pennsylvania in Indiana, PA. I pursued my interest in art and earned a Bachelor of Fine Arts Degree. I married Sharon, my college girlfriend, and we had a beautiful, healthy son named Ryan, on June 19, 1986. I was determined to give Ryan the childhood I didn't get to have.

Having recently graduated, and with no job offers beating down my door, I decided to join the United States Navy to help provide a better life for my new family. Sharon and I moved to Charleston, South Carolina, where I was stationed. I quickly rose to higher ranks in the three years I served in the Navy.

The service was good to me. I learned many valuable life lessons while there. They taught me courage, dedication, commitment, honor, team work, and responsibility. These are qualities I still believe in.

However, being away at sea so much didn't help bind together a new marriage. Sharon and I divorced in 1991. I was in a tailspin trying to establish a career, spend time with my son, and put my life back together. I worked at several small retail companies, working my way up to store manager very quickly until I was offered a steady management position in 1994 with a company called Service Merchandise, and moved to Ohio.

I met my current wife, Carolyn, in 1994 while working there. We married in 2000. In 2004, we were blessed with a beautiful, healthy baby girl named Elena. I then began moving through the ranks of retail management, and had a great career working as a store manager for several Fortune 500 retail companies.

Life was good. I had a promising career, a wonderful family, a beautiful home, and lived close to where my parents still lived in Greenville, PA. I would make time to visit Mom, Dad, and Aunt Sandi, as well as friends from the neighborhood as often as I could work around my very busy manager's schedule.

I hardly ever thought about my life in Korea over those twenty years. I was so busy with work, family, and friends that I never let myself go back to that dark time when I was unsure I would ever find happiness or the love and security of a family. I think in many ways I was good at blocking out the negative times in my life and only focusing on what was in front of me. It is what kept me moving forward. I never stopped to dwell in the past, or worried about changing things that could no longer be changed. Everything about my personality drove me to always look forward and think about how I could make my life, and the lives of others around me, better in the future.

I truly felt comfortable, safe, and loved. I felt like I had finally gotten to a good place in my life and that everything was going to be just fine from then on. Unfortunately, God had other plans.

Chapter 16

Losing

Mom called me in October of 2008 and told me that Dad had to see the doctor about some persistent heartburn problems he was experiencing. Dad remained his usual busy self, playing organ at the church every week and dedicating himself to musical events of all kinds. He was gearing up for his busy season, conducting the Messiah at the Presbyterian Church in Greenville like he had done every Christmas for the past thirty-six years. He was constantly running here and there from one musical event to another, never slowing down even after retiring in 1997 after teaching public school for twenty-eight years. He was always full of energy as his genuine passion for music shone through at each event where he either conducted or played flute, piano, organ, trombone, or recorder.

That's why when the doctor called with the results of his physical tests and said that he had stage IV esophageal cancer, we were all caught off guard. Outside of the heartburn episodes, there was no real indication that cancer had been quietly growing inside him.

We were all devastated. Dad, however, remained his usual cheery self, and told us all not to worry. Four short months later, on February 4, 2009, Dad died.

I was devastated. Here was the only father I had ever known, and a great one at that. He was only sixty-seven years old. I had planned on spending many more years with him. He adored his grandchildren, and loved spending time watching them grow up. Mom stayed strong throughout his battle, but I know it was the most difficult thing she had ever been through. They had been together for forty years and had a close bond that some couples only dream about.

After all the years of blocking out tragedy from my life, I wasn't sure how to comprehend this one. I had been so young when I had been separated from my biological family that it was easy to close the door to that pain and move forward. This, however, was a whole new kind of pain. It was very fresh and very sudden. I kept thinking of all the different ways I wished I could have been a better son, or spent more time with him instead of doing other things that seemed so trivial now. I had lost the man who was the true inspiration and guiding force in my life. I had tried to model my behavior and ethics after this man that I idolized and respected.

I spent as much time as I could with Mom, my brother David, and Aunt Sandi even with my hectic work schedule. I knew that Mom and Aunt Sandi were both strong women and would pull through it together. Dad had always encouraged us to find strength in all of life's many challenges. Because of that, I knew I had to find a healthy way to cope with my immeasurable grief.

Chapter 17

Finding Jin

In the three years following Dad's unexpected death, I found many ways to distract myself. I started a part-time business as a motivational speaker. When people found out my background, and how I always managed to stay focused on the positive, it seemed like a natural transition to me to spread that enthusiasm for life to others. I started my motivational speaking company, JSSTEARNS ENTERPRISES (www.jsstearnsenterprises.com) in September, 2010. I spoke at various church and business organizations on how to tackle the obstacles in your life and move forward better and stronger than you thought possible. I continued to work full-time in retail management and spend time with my wife and daughter, and visit my son Ryan, who was living in South Carolina. Ryan made me a grandfather in April of 2011, and I was now the proud Grandpa of a happy, bouncing baby boy named Kai Stearns. Except for losing Dad, my life could not have been more stable again. At this point in my life, I was content.

However, contentment is not necessarily synonymous with fulfillment. There just seemed to be something nagging at me, almost welling up from within me, as if it had been repressed for so long that it needed to be set free. I began letting my mind drift back to my life in Korea. I was now nearing fifty years old, and realized I had not had any desire to go back to Korea during the past forty years. Thoughts of Korea and my first ten years of life now became stronger, and started occurring more often. I had always been curious about what had happened to my brothers, Kyang Soo and Yae Soo, but had never really felt a drive to delve back into my past. I had always appeased my anxiety about them by thinking that they had good lives and were not thinking about me, either.

I think the death of my beloved father, and the fact that I was nearing forty years away from my homeland, triggered feelings in me of curiosity and longing for answers to my past. I think it became hard for me to realize that I was going to be fifty years old in December of 2012, and I still did not have any clue as to who I was for the first ten years of my life. I knew who I had become, and was secure with myself in that knowledge. But my mind kept wandering back to the past, to my childhood, if you could call it that, and to what events had happened in Korea to lead me to this place in my life and to be the person that I am today.

Chapter 18

Finding My Brothers

One harsh lesson that I learned after losing my father so quickly to cancer is that life is truly short. For the past forty years, I had considered going back to Korea and searching for my brothers as something that could always wait "until there was a better time." It seemed like there was always some other life event occupying my time and attention, and that it was never the "right" time.

After losing Dad, I realized that time is something that we have no control over. It seems there will always be something more pressing or "more important" coming and going throughout our lives, so to try to prepare for an event to happen at the "right" time becomes more and more illogical. We have no way of knowing what our future holds from one day to the next. One thing I have definitely learned from my father's death is that we work on God's time, not our own!

I also had to admit one more thing to myself before I could go any further with my thoughts of returning to Korea: I was afraid. I was afraid for many reasons. I was going back to a place where I had repressed so many abrupt and tragic memories, and was scared of what I would find had become of my biological family. It felt safer to live in oblivion and convince myself that both of my brothers had fared well in their lives and thought of me no more than I did of them and our childhood; maybe just as a passing curiosity from time to time.

However, one day in early February of 2012, my friend Gina, who is originally from Korea and had been living in the United States for the past thirty years, called to say she was planning a trip back to Korea to see her family. She said if we ever wanted to go to Korea, now would be a good time. I did not know what to say. I wasn't sure about booking such a major trip, but over a few weeks, my wife convinced me that it would be a once in a lifetime opportunity. So with that, we booked a flight for me, my wife, and my daughter. Gina would fly over with us on the same flight, bringing her two American-born daughters for their first-time journey to Korea as well.

In the same time period that I was booking the tickets and making plans for the trip, a thought had come to me. A few new Facebook friends from GOAL (a website for post-Korean adoptees to chit chat) had been to Korea in the past, and had mentioned that there was a TV show in Korea called *I Miss That Person*. The show helped families in Korea to search for and reconnect with lost loved ones. My GOAL friends told me that there was a long waiting list since hundreds of requests are received every year to the Korean Broadcasting Station (KBS), and they can only select a limited number of requests per year for a live broadcast. So, although I knew it was difficult to get on the show, I decided I had nothing to lose by just submitting my story to them to see if they would possibly be interested.

Following are some of the emails I exchanged with the staff who work for KBS:

Sat, Apr 7, 2012

Dear Mr. Ho Hwan Choi,

I hope this letter finds you well. My name is Jin Stearns (Korean: Kim Jin Soo), and I humbly ask your help in a matter that is of most importance to my life. An American family in the United States adopted me from Holt Orphanage in Korea in 1973. Before I came to America, I had two older brothers whom I got separated from at a train station when I was 6 years old. I was placed in the orphanage and never saw or heard from them again.

It has been my dream for the last 40 years to be reunited with them; however, I have no information about them except for their names: Kim Kyang Soo and Kim Yae Soo. I am planning my first trip ever back to Korea in July 6–20, 2012 and would be honored if you would be able to help me through your show. I am hoping that if I am able to appear on your show and tell my story, my brothers (if they are watching) may recognize me (from my pictures when I was 8) and contact your station. I have no other way of finding them since I have no more information about them.

I know you have a lot of people waiting who you are helping in similar situations, and I can only ask you to please understand how important this is to me. I have never been able to get back to Korea until now. It would be such a miracle to have you help with my search, and to finally be able to let them know what happened to me all those years ago, and that I'm doing fine. I have a wonderful family and a great life, and my son and daughter would love to meet their uncles.

I have attached my adoption records from Holt Orphanage for you to review. Please let me know if there are any questions or if we can speak further about this. My Korean language is not the greatest. You can contact me through my email address or my business website at www.jsstearnsenterprises.com

Thank you for your time and attention to my request and God Bless.

Respectfully,

Jin Stearns

May 25, 2012

Dear Mr. Jin Stearns,

This is Lucia Hong from new producing team.

We now know that you are visiting Korea from July 6 to July 20.

Our program will be broadcast live on every Friday. That means July 6th, 13th, and 20th.

While you are visiting Korea, you can contact us.

We cannot guarantee that you will surely be on the program but considering your schedule, it is highly probable.

We really hope that you will be on the program and find your brothers.

Warm regards

Lucia Hong

May 29, 2012

Hi Lucia—

I thank you so much for the consideration. You have no idea what this means to me. I personally would like to thank everyone at your Station when I'm there (Korea) in July. God bless.

Jin Stearns

June 19, 2012

Dear Mr. Stearns

I've finished translating all your interview questionnaire and adoption file from English to Korean.

Your story was very moving and impressive. Thank you for sharing your story.

The producing crew are really interested in your story and they want to give you longer time among our main quests by showing longer videos of you and your story before your live interview.

If you can come to the show on July 20th, the producing crew said, you will be given a longer time in a live program.

When you come to Korea, before broadcasting, the film crew can arrange the schedule with you to shoot your trace such as the orphanages where you were and the train station where you were separated from your older brothers.

We really hope you will be on the show and find your brothers through this program.

I have some questions to ask to you.

1) You said you are going to stay here from July 6th until July 20th. We would like to know the exact schedule. We first thought that it would be good for you to be on TV on July 13th. But on July 13th other main guest is expected to be given longer time.

Is it okay for you to be on the live show on July 20th 11:00am Friday?

If not, please let me know.

2) When I read your interview answers, you said the birth date is given by Holt, which means it is estimated?

3) Do you remember the name of the train station where you and your brothers were separated?

The adoption file said it was Seoul Railroad Station. Do you think it is right? I thought so because back in 1960s Seoul Railroad Station was the most crowded station, I heard.

I will be waiting for your reply.

With kind regards,

Lucia Hong

June 23, 2012

Dear Mr. Stearns,

On July 13th, you will be one of our 4 main guests, and the producing crew said if you can be on TV on July 20th you will be the mainest of our main guests by giving you longer time (5 minutes more) showing more videos of you and your story.

Each main guest is given more or less 11 minutes of interview.

The producing crew will have a meeting on Monday to decide whether you would be broadcast on July 20th which I think is highly likely.

I wonder if it is okay to let you know on Monday and if you still would like to delay the flight schedule.

KBS is a national broadcasting company so our program schedule is so much affected by national events such as election or Olympic events.

We have presidential election ahead this year so we have primary elections in the summer

Last Friday, because of primaries of one party, our program scheduled on June 22 couldn't be on TV.

We will try our best to prepare our program, but also we would like you to know the program schedule can be affected, which is the last thing we want.

If the program is broadcast on schedule, it would be great for you to delay your flight schedule.

We hope that this program will be broadcast on schedule and most of all we really hope you would meet your brothers.

I will email you about the meeting on Monday.

If you have any question, feel free to call or email me.

With best regards

Lucia Hong

June 25, 2012

Dear Stearns,

Thank you for sending many precious pictures and videos.
You had a very beautiful family.

The producing crew decided today that you would be our mainest of our main guests on July 13th.

You will be given longer time among our main guests.

Maybe your story will cover over a third of the entire program on that day.

I know you will arrive in Korea on July 6th and you are supposed to visit Holt Orphanage on July 9th.

The film crew wants to shoot your video of you vising your traces in Korea. (Maybe the orphanages where you were and the Seoul Railroad Station where you were separated from your brothers and etc.)

The filming date would be one day among three days from July7th to July9th. (July 9th Monday would be highly likely.)

And the important request to you.

We (me and the producing crew) want you to stay until July 20th.

Since you remember your brothers' name correctly, it is thought highly possible that you will reunite with your brothers. We really hope that after your broadcast on July 13th, we would get calls from your brothers.

We can't say for sure but in case your brothers give calls to the team within the week, we would like you to stay until July 20th when you might appear again on the program if you reunite with them.

That means we want you to delay your flight schedule by one day.

We will be waiting for your reply.

With best regards,

Lucia Hong

June 27, 2012

Lucia—

Thank you for all you do. We are very much looking forward to meeting you and your crew July 7th @ 4 p.m. at the airport!!!!

Warm regards,

Jin Stearns

Chapter 19

The Present Meets the Past

Our trip to Korea was set. I was beyond excited. We had planned on leaving Cleveland on July 6, 2012, and arriving in Incheon, South Korea at 4 p.m. on the seventh. We would have a two week stay in Korea in which I could search for my brothers, reconnect with my heritage, and explore the amazing landscapes and culture with my wife and daughter.

As my wife Carolyn, daughter Elena and I boarded the plane to Korea with Gina and her daughters, I was flooded with a range of emotions. I did not know what to expect. Rather than get my hopes up, I decided to expect nothing. I would keep an open mind with no preconceived notions about what Korea may be like, and I certainly would not let myself entertain the idea that it would be easy to find and reconnect with my brothers. I knew nothing about them anymore except for their names. I did not know what had become of them: if they were still living in Korea at all; if they, too, had gone to orphanages and had been adopted to other countries; if they were even still together; if they were looking for me; if they had any contact with either of our parents; or if they were even still alive. There were just too many possibilities for me to try to wrap my mind around. All I could do was pray that God would lead me to the answers to these questions I had long ago suppressed in my mind, and that He would give me the strength to accept the answers when and if they came.

The flight was long, but my family and I were so excited it seemed that we had no time to feel tired. We flew from Cleveland to Chicago, then changed planes to fly non-stop from Chicago to Incheon. There was a mileage indicator on a TV screen on the seat in front of me, and I watched as the miles ticked away and we soared closer and closer to our destination. We were over 6,000 miles away from Canton, Ohio, the place I now called home.

My nerves were starting to kick in a little when the pilot announced that we would be landing in Incheon in just minutes. Carolyn was making me laugh because she pointed out that we needed to "look fresh" for the KBS cameras after we had just spent sixteen hours on airplanes with no shower or fresh change of clothes. The cameras were already arranged to be waiting for us at the airport, so all we had to do once we landed was get our luggage, go out the doors, and be met with a camera crew filming my first step onto Korean soil in decades.

Easier said than done, I guess. After we landed, went through customs, and collected our luggage, we exited out the closest door to the baggage claim area. We waited for the popping of flashbulbs and the whirring of cameras that we had envisioned. There was nothing. No media, no press, no one with a microphone; only throngs of people holding up signs and waiting for their loved ones.

My first thought was that we had been dumped by the TV show, and we just did not get the message since we were on planes for the last sixteen hours and unable to receive messages. Then Carolyn asked if maybe there was another exit. I wandered several yards to the other side of the airport, and sure enough, there was a second arrival gate.

Waiting there with cameras and microphones were Lucia Hong and two cameramen from KBS.

I was now approaching them from behind, rather than coming through the gates for them to film me. They were startled when I tapped Lucia on the shoulder to introduce myself. She explained that they had been waiting there awhile, and were puzzled when we did not come through the gates with the rest of the passengers from our flight. I felt terrible that I had messed up the moment that they had planned so carefully, but was grateful that they were there after all, and that they were still planning on filming my story for the show.

Lucia was wonderful about the whole incident, and arranged with the airport security for us to go back through the arrival doors and stage the scene as if we had just arrived through the gates. They continued to film us as we walked to an awaiting airport bus to take us to our hotel, interviewing me the whole way about my thoughts and feelings about returning to Korea after so long.

Thankfully, Lucia spoke both English and Korean, because the first thing that impacted me was the language barrier. In all my time in the United States, I never had a time when I needed to use the Korean language again. I had forgotten how to read, write, listen to, and speak my own native tongue. I had not heard Korean for a while, but had thought as soon as I was immersed back into it, it all would just come back to me in a tidal wave. I was sorely mistaken. As I looked at the signs in the airport and listened to people freely conversing, I was lost. I could only make out the most fundamental of words like *hello, yes*, and *no*.

I was actually slightly uncomfortable, because all the feelings of helplessness I felt when I first arrived in the

United States when I was ten years old came flooding back to me. It was so ironic that, almost forty years ago to the day, I would be in the same situation where I was unable to understand and communicate because I did not know the language. However, this time, instead of being fluent in Korean and then submersed into an English-speaking environment, now I was fluent in English, and submersed into a Korean-speaking environment. God must have a sense of humor, but I was not laughing!

Luckily, after we left the airport and settled into our hotel, we contacted Gina, who had been picked up at the airport by her nephew and was staying with her family not far from our hotel. Although Gina had lived in the USA for the past thirty years, she still remained active in Korean circles and never lost her ability to speak and write the language. So for the first week of our stay in Korea, we were treated to the incomparable hospitality of Gina's family, starting at breakfast and lasting all day, until they dropped us off at our hotel late at night.

Gina's family introduced us to all different cultural aspects of Korea, starting with the food. Her youngest brother, Chong Ho, would pick us up at the hotel early in the morning before he left for work and take us to his house to spend the day with his family. We would enjoy a traditional Korean breakfast consisting of many varieties of kimchee, rice, soups and other delicacies. Lunch would be either at the house, or at one of the many delicious Korean restaurants nearby. Dinner was always at a very nice restaurant, in which most of the time the food was cooked right at the table as everyone gathered around and ate out of community dishes with their chopsticks. On one occasion, it was Chong Ho's birthday, so we were treated to seaweed soup for breakfast. That is the most traditional part of a birthday when you are older in Korea, as the rest of the day is more low-key and downplayed. There are no flashy birthday celebrations or parties like in the USA. Instead, there are quiet family dinners and the exchange of a modest gift or two.

A person's age in Korea is also one year more than their age would be in the United States. In Korea, on the day of your birth, you are already considered to be one year old, as the time spent in the womb is counted toward your age.

The birthdays in Korea that are truly significant are the first day of your birth, followed by the more important "100-Days Birthday." Because throughout Korean history babies would often fall sick and die, it became a major event if a baby lived past 100 days. Therefore, the 100-days birthday became the biggest marker of a person's rate of survival. After this milestone, a person had a better chance of living into adulthood.

Some families in Korean history even planned a special name for their child to help ensure a better rate of survival. Korea is heavily influenced by beliefs in supernatural forces, and many thought it was because of evil spirits that a baby would fall ill and die in infancy. Therefore, in order to trick the evil spirits, people would name their child an unattractive name such as Daegee, which means "pig" in Korean. The belief was that the evil spirits would bypass a child with a name like "pig" as an undesirable, thus protecting the child from an early death.

The most interesting custom we were introduced to in Korea was the removal of our shoes. Before anyone enters a house or certain business places in Korea, shoes are removed and left in a front area similar to an American mudroom. If you are in a hotel room or restaurant, then house slippers resembling sturdy flip flops are provided at the entrance for guests or patrons to wear. When you are ready to leave, your shoes can be retrieved at the front area, and often have been stacked neatly onto shelves by staff. The reason for this custom is that Korean culture is very conscientious of how much dirt can be dragged in on one's shoes, and removing them before entering a building helps to keep living areas more clean and sanitary. Although not every restaurant or business in Korea practices this custom today, we were exposed to it enough times to become familiar with the practice, and soon it became automatic to slide off our shoes the moment we entered a domicile or place of business. My wife and I were almost disappointed when we would occasionally visit an area where taking off our shoes was not required. It was such a distinct part of Korean culture, and we enjoyed feeling like a native when we were able to partake in the custom. I had become so Americanized that I had forgotten all the ways of Korean culture that I was now re-experiencing. Living in an orphanage all those years kept me in a confined environment where I really didn't get to know and appreciate the ways of other Koreans around me.

Gina's family took us to different areas of Korea for sightseeing, including Min Sok Chon, a huge Korean cultural park in Yujin City. Gina had been staying with her sister in a different area of Korea, so Carolyn, Elena, and I had to take a bus from Incheon to Yujin City (about an hour and a half away) to meet them at Min Sok Chon. We managed to get all the way to Yujin City with no problems, until the bus dropped us off at the stop where we were supposed to catch a taxi to make the short distance over to the park. That is when I most noticed how little I knew of reading and speaking the Korean language. I was frustrated because there did not seem to be any taxis passing by, so we decided to walk up the street. A little ways up was a police station, so we stopped in to ask for directions. However, there was only one officer who spoke a little English, and it was difficult for us to communicate what we wanted. When they figured out we wanted to go to Min Sok Chon, they told us to wait. We didn't know what was going on, or if we were in trouble, but a few minutes later, a police car pulled up, with an officer who spoke more English. He explained to us that Min Sok Chon was only a few miles away, and that he would take us there. I was really impressed with the kindness that was shown to us by the police officers. It is such a helpless feeling to be lost and not able to communicate, and their kindness for tourists was much appreciated. Imagine Gina's surprise when we pulled up to the gate to meet them at Min Sok Chon and stepped out of the back of a police car!

* * *

I was smitten with Korea. In one short week, I felt like I had been mesmerized by the beauty of the land and the grace of the people. Gorgeous mountains with rolling fog bordered wide-stretching sandy beaches, all topped off with the grandiose architecture of ancient Korean temples and statues. Most every area and angle of Korea was breathtaking. I had a hard time believing I was back there, and that I was in places I had never before knew existed. Korea, to me, was pure magic.

Chapter 20

Chasing the Dream

For all the time I spent engaged in reconnecting with the people and culture of Korea, I never lost sight of the real focus for my trip: finding my brothers. On Monday, July 9, I had an appointment with Mrs. Lee of Holt Adoption Services. I wanted to go over the file they had on me to see if there was any information that could aid me in my search. KBS also wanted to film me as I made a return to the train station where I had so many years ago been separated from my brothers. Gina's sister-in-law drove my wife, daughter, and me from Incheon to Seoul (about an hour's drive) to meet up with Lucia Hong and the camera crew once again.

We met in what is now the modern day Seoul Train Station terminal. It was a monstrous concoction of steel and glass, and it was overwhelming in its size as well as the number of people rushing in and out on their various journeys. Lucia asked me jokingly if I recognized it and I said, "No, but I was a lot smaller then." Of course I would not remember this new terminal because it was built in 2004, thirty-one years after I had left Korea. Then Lucia pointed to the left at an older building that stopped me in my tracks (no pun intended). There it was, not more than fifty yards away: the original Seoul Train Station. The place where so long ago, I thought my life had ended when I lost my Korean family. But also the place where my life truly began as it became the first step in my future with my American family. I wondered how one place could bring so much tragedy, yet so much joy, all at the same time. I thought my life was over when I was lost, but now I realized that it was the turning point that shaped me into the man that I am today. I looked at it with mixed feelings of sadness, longing, and regret, all that were soon washed away with the relief and understanding that God had chosen a wonderful path for my life that I could never have envisioned hiding under that bench all those years ago.

We slowly made our way over to the old train station, which had signs posted around it announcing that it was closed to visitors as it was undergoing reconstruction and remodeling to preserve it as a future historical cultural site. I was extremely disappointed. I had really wanted to go inside and look around. Some part of me wanted to stand in the last place that I had seen my brothers; to make me feel like I was a part of them again. Luckily, my wife has very little patience for being closed out of things and decided to take action. Peering through the window and seeing a security guard inside, she motioned for him to come closer so we could talk to him. Since he only spoke Korean, and we did not, Carolyn asked Lucia to tell him our situation and see if we could look around for a few brief moments. Lucia was doubtful that it would be favorable since the signs said the area was definitely closed to visitors, but my wife was insistent. She told Lucia that we did not travel six thousand miles just to be stopped by a closed sign. So Lucia reluctantly explained to the guard our purpose for disturbing him, and he told us to wait just a moment. He made a few calls on his walkie-talkie, and after what seemed a long time, opened the door widely and invited us in. He had contacted the people in charge of the building, and they graciously allowed us in to look around and do our filming. It actually worked out better than if it had been open for visitors, because now we had the place all to ourselves. It was quiet, humongous, and every bit as overwhelming as I remembered it as a small boy in 1968. Feelings of fear and excitement mingled inside me and made my stomach do flip flops.

As we entered the main doors, I held my breath. My mind flashed back to all those many years ago, and for an instant, I felt like that same lost little boy again. Although the halls and rooms were now well-worn and deserted, it gave me chills to be in the cavernous entryway where so many people had hustled and bustled on their daily journeys to everywhere. Our footsteps across the pristine granite floor echoed off the high stone walls as we meandered down the symmetrical halls until we reached the great dome at the main entrance in the center of the building. The Byzantine-style dome, paired with the granite floors and stone columns and walls, made the station a breathtaking view of simplistic elegance.

I slowly walked down the expansive hallway to my right, quietly taking in the beautiful architecture and the cleanliness of such an old landmark. As I walked further ahead, I saw to my right something that sparked a flood of memories for me, even though the old railway tracks were enclosed by a glass wall to prevent anyone from entering as the restoration process was taking place. As I glanced to my left at that section of the tracks, my knees suddenly went weak when I realized where I was.

I was standing in the corner of the train station, directly across from the tracks, in the exact spot where I had lost my brother all those many years ago. It is a memory that would stick with me forever, and I had no doubt about it. This was the spot. It was missing the bench that I had hid under and cried for so long after I realized that I was all alone, but it still *felt* the same. As I stood in the corner, transfixed, I was transformed to the past where I was once again that little six-year-old boy who was so frightened and alone, cowering under the bench in the hopes that no one would see me until I was found by my family.

Tears welled up in my eyes, and I gently removed my glasses to brush them away. I have never been one to outwardly express my feelings, and my wife had never seen me cry before in all of our years of marriage, not even through the deaths of loved ones. She began to cry upon seeing how much this moment impacted me. Lost in our own emotions, we had all but forgotten that the KBS cameras were on us, filming our every reaction for the TV show. I could recall the depth of pain from 40 years ago like it was yesterday when I had lost my brother here in this very spot. Overcome with emotion and confusion by all of this, my little daughter came over and wrapped her arms around my waist to try to comfort me. It was a hard day for all of us, and the camera crew caught it all on tape. I did not want to linger any longer, and breathed a deep sigh of relief as we walked hand in hand back out the doors and into the sunshine of Seoul.

Chapter 21

Post-Adoption Answers

I had an appointment for 4:00 p.m. at the Holt Post-Adoption Services Center in another section of Seoul, so Gina's sister-in-law, who had been shopping in the modern shopping center near the Seoul Train Station, swung by to pick us up and drive us to our meeting. Lucia and the camera crew rode along in the van, interviewing and filming us for the entire twenty minute drive.

When we reached the building, I was even more eager to find out all I could about my past. I had just had a deeply emotional experience in the train station where I had lost my family, and I was more ready than ever to erase that pain by trying to reunite with my brothers. I was filled with excitement and hope as I entered the doors of the Holt Post-Adoption Services Center.

In the entryway, we were all instructed to remove our shoes and put on house slippers before we were escorted to the elevator by an elderly gentleman who appeared to be the door greeter. As the elevator doors opened onto the fourth floor, my heart was racing with anticipation of what new information I may learn about my past.

Mrs. Lee, my assigned caseworker, met us in the hallway and led us to a small conference room down a short hall. My wife, daughter, and I were seated on one side of the table with Mrs. Lee across from us. It was warm in the room, and we were offered cool water as we waited for my file to be brought in. I had brought some paperwork of my own that I had requested from the main Holt International offices in Eugene, Oregon several months back when I was still in the United States.

I felt like I had a million questions for Mrs. Lee. However, to my disappointment, no new answers were provided. When my file was brought in, we realized that it contained the exact same information that I had in my own file from Oregon. I asked Mrs. Lee if there was any way anyone from the orphanage would remember anything more, but she was not very encouraging. I got the impression that I was just one more name in a sea of people who came through there looking for answers to their past, only no answers were there. After the rush of emotions I had experienced when standing in the train station less than an hour ago, I couldn't believe that I was no closer to finding my Korean family than I had been forty- three years earlier. Dejected, I shook hands with Mrs. Lee, who wished me luck in my search, and then headed back down the elevator and into the waiting van to take us back to our hotel.

* * *

Later, I tried to wrap my mind around all the events that had happened that day. I felt like I was on an emotional roller coaster, with my hopes going up and down with every new twist and turn of my journey back to Korea. For every step I moved forward toward finding answers, it felt like I was cruelly pushed ten steps back. I began to wonder what I was doing, and if all of this was more than I could handle. I was disappointed by the lack of new information from my appointment earlier, yet I was still clinging to the hope that I would be appearing on KBS TV on Friday to tell my story to the whole country. Surely, I thought, that could be a major opening to get my story out there and maybe, just maybe, my Korean family would be watching and call the station.

I should have learned from all the unpredictability in my life not to put all my eggs into one basket.

* * *

Just when I thought I was down, Gina called on Tuesday morning with amazing news. She said she had just spoken to her second youngest brother, Byeong-Su, and that he had some friends that worked in the police department in Incheon. He wanted her to bring me to the police station during his lunch hour so that I could give all my information to the police. He felt that with both the police and the TV station working to locate my brothers, we would have better odds of finding them.

It took over an hour and a half to give the police a thoroughly detailed description of what few events in my life I recalled that could lead them to my brothers. The best lead that they had to go on was that I had still managed to remember the names of my brothers. It was very unusual for someone to be named Yae Soo, which means "Jesus" in Korean, even for a family who was devout Christian. In a country where Buddhism was a dominant religion, it made the name all the more puzzling. However, this was good news to me. The more chance I had of narrowing down the field, the better chances I thought I had of finding Yae Soo and Kyang Soo.

Chapter 22

Going "Home"

While reconnecting with my roots in Korea, one of the goals I had was to go back and visit the place where I had spent time in my young life: Holt Orphanage in Ilsan. I had also had a somewhat morbid interest in seeing if there were remains of my first orphanage, Hwa Saeng Won, but was secretly relieved when I was told that since its closure in 1972, there was really no way to find out anything more about it. I was excited, though, to try to visit Holt Ilsan, which played a huge role in my development into the person I am today. Holt Ilsan is still located in Gyeonggi-do, Goyang, South Korea.

I knew very little about the present-day Holt Ilsan Center, except for what I had been able to research on the internet before my trip to Korea. It seemed that Holt Ilsan Center no longer housed all orphans as it had when I was a resident. Now it was a special care facility only for orphans who had special needs, and who were not very likely to ever be adopted. When I was there, it was only for children; today, Holt Ilsan cares for all mentally and physically disabled residents from babies to adults. There are currently around 300 residents, some of whom started there as infants and were hard to adopt out due to their multiple special needs, and then just continued to stay on at the Ilsan facility for the remainder of their lives. All the other orphans under Holt's care who are not considered to have special needs were now placed with foster mothers all over Korea, much like we do in the United States. As of 2010, Holt Children Services was credited for finding loving, permanent homes for 101,981 children. Harry Holt, the founder of Holt International, a Christian organization, had the belief that "Every Child Deserves a Home."

Even if people cannot commit to adopting a child, help can still be given through this organization by sponsoring a child until they could be adopted. My church in the United States recently became a sponsor through Holt of a little baby named Min Ju, who was being cared for by a foster mother in Seoul until she could be adopted by a family of her own. I had it on my to-do list while in Korea to visit Min Ju and take pictures of her to share with the church.

Since I did not want to show up at the Holt Ilsan Center entirely unannounced, I decided to call the orphanage on the morning of July 10 to see if it would be alright for me to come by and visit. I was pleasantly surprised when I called to be handed over directly to Molly Holt herself. Molly is one of the biological daughters of Harry and Bertha Holt, and is the chairperson of Holt Children's Services. She continues to dedicate her life to running the Holt Ilsan facilities and personally caring for the orphans.

Molly had a kind voice over the phone, and I couldn't wait to meet her. She sincerely invited me to stop by that afternoon to spend time touring the facilities. She said she was not often at Ilsan due to having to travel around Korea and to the United States to do work for Holt International, but that my timing was perfect. She would be there all afternoon that day. Although I didn't tell Molly at the time, today's date, July 10, had more than one meaning for me. It was on the same day back in 1972 that I had arrived in New York City as an adoptee from Holt Ilsan to begin my new life in America. How ironic to go back on that day, to the very place that had put my new life in motion.

Molly's kindness was the just the encouragement I needed to face the task of returning to the memories of my childhood. I could vividly recall the love, kindness, and care that Holt showered upon me as a child, and I was afraid that if I went back, I would see that the reality was not the same as what I had chosen to remember all those years.

Luckily, all that worrying was for nothing. As I pulled up to the gates of the Holt Ilsan Center, I recognized the entrance right away. It was definitely more weathered, and some areas were either new or rebuilt, but the feel of it was still the same: I felt safe. From the moment I entered the gate and stepped into the doors of the welcome center, all the staff was kind and greeted me like a long-lost friend, even though most of them were young and could not have been working there when I was a resident. But the unequivocally best part of the experience was the warm greeting I received from Molly.

She was exactly as I had imagined her to be. She was short with gray hair, and had a kind and gentle face; one marked with years of putting others' care and concern above her own. She reminded me of a sweet, welcoming grandmother, and I felt as if I had known her all my life. She wrapped her arms around me in a warm hug as she told me how nice it was of me to have traveled so far. She asked if we had eaten lunch, and offered my wife, daughter and I a place at the table as they were just about to sit down to eat. This is the customary greeting in Korea that extends way back into Korean history. During the time period when Koreans were very poor and did not have much to eat, it was common upon meeting someone to ask "Have you eaten?" rather than "How are you" as is the custom in American culture. It was a way to be considerate and show concern for those who may not have had any food during times when food was scarce, and the greeting has carried on into present day.

We were in the cozy dining room of the modest building where Molly also housed her tiny office. She explained to us that it was the only building left that her father, Harry, had originally built. There were several residents and volunteers gathered around an oblong wooden table. I was touched as to how Molly was so truly integrated into the lives of her staff and residents. She helped feed some residents herself, and was continually making sure everyone had all they needed to be comfortable. It made my heart swell to realize that all the compassion and love I felt as an orphan so long ago was still there, and in such a humble and genuine way.

Since we had already eaten before we came, we declined lunch, but were happy to sit on the nearby loveseat and pore over the photo albums that Molly gave us to look through. I was happy to learn that she was bilingual. I could understand her easily, and knew that when she spoke to the residents in their native Korean, she was able to make everyone feel at such ease. She had albums from many years, and gave us the one from 1972, a year that I would have been living there. Just looking through it gave me shivers as I saw many buildings and scenery that was so much a part of my past. One picture that drew my wife's attention was that of several young boys standing around a dirt field and talking. One boy was holding a bag, and another was on an old bicycle. The shot was taken from a hill above, somewhat far away, so that you were looking down at the boys. Instantly, I knew that the boy with the bag was me. It was so amazing that there was a picture of me as a child in Korea. I had never seen photos of myself growing up in Korea except for the required entrance and exit photos taken at the orphanage from my adoption file. It was the first time I had seen a candid shot of me in a natural setting, and it made me happy. Molly later told us that it was so hard back then to adopt out older boys, and again, I felt blessed that Frank and Pat Stearns had opened their hearts and their home to choose me out of all the boys in that photo.

Photo from Molly Holt's scrapbook taken in 1972. I am the boy holding the bag directly above the boy on the bike.

When we finished looking through the albums, and Molly had finished with lunch, she sat on the couch and shared stories of what the orphanage had been like in the past and how it was today. Her voice was filled with passion for carrying on her parent's mission to help orphans all around the world. In fact, it was because of the dedication and compassion of Harry and Bertha Holt that international adoption became a reality in places like the United States. The Holts' calling to bring home eight orphaned Korean babies after the Korean War helped break down barriers and open the floodgates to international adoption for families in the United States. I will be forever grateful to the Holts for saving me from my first orphanage, showing me via the great care they took of me when at Ilsan that love and caring did exist in the world, and for creating the pathway that allowed me to be adopted to the United States by a wonderful family who truly loved me.

Molly, who was born in America, said that she came to Korea when she was just twenty years old, and coincidentally, to Busan, the city of my birth. While she was taken with the beauty and kindness of the Korean people, she returned to the USA to attend college to further her studies, and became a missionary for the next ten years. She became the director for Holt in Korea in 1967, when they housed approximately 750 orphans.

Molly made it a point to study Korean so that she could learn it properly. Too often, she explained, if you try to learn Korean on your own, you may only pick up what is considered "low language," and you are more likely to unintentionally insult people when you speak. The Korean language is a source of deep pride within the history of the country. As a matter of fact, the written language was deliberately created from scratch, rather than developing naturally on its own. In 1446, King Sejong of the Yi Dynasty was concerned about the lack of literacy in Korea. The language spoken at the time was Chinese, and since it was such a complex language, most of the people in the lower social classes (non-aristocrats) were unable to read or write it. King Sejong decided to create a much simpler language using some of the foundations of the Chinese language, so that everyone could learn to read and write. This new language was called Hangul, and consisted of a twenty-four-letter alphabet and words written in simple syllables. The language maintained the most important aspect of Korean culture: respect for elder members of the society. The words chosen to address someone through conversation emphasized either a polite form or a familiar form, so that when you spoke, proper respect was apparent in your words.

Molly traveled back and forth from Korea to the United States during those ten years, particularly to come back for the funeral of her father, Harry. When I told Molly that Holt had rescued me from a terrible orphanage that later closed down, she said that she was not surprised. Because of the Korean War from 1950—1953, there became an influx of orphans all around Korea. Some children became orphans after their fathers and other family members were killed during the war, while others became orphans during the American occupation after the war had already ended. American GIs fathered children with Korean women, which were given up to orphanages. There was no greater shame in Korean culture at the time than to be a bi-racial child. Shunned by society, they were considered the lowest class of orphans. Because there seemed to be an endless supply of orphans during this time frame, many unethical orphanages sprang up just to make money off of the misfortunes of children. Molly confirmed that some orphanages at the time were not as good as others, and I believe that Hwa Saeng Won fit into that category. Molly said that Holt had tried to take in as many children as they could as these shady organizations were folding, and I again realized how lucky I was that Holt had been there when I needed them.

I asked her if she knew anything about the incident in my records where a lady had come to Holt claiming to be a relative of mine. Molly said maybe it was a good thing that I did not go with her because back then it was common for people to go to orphanages and claim to be some type of relative, only to get children to work on their farms. No other information was given about the woman, not even a name, and Molly felt badly that such sloppy work had been done at the time.

* * *

While we were sitting and talking, Molly introduced me to Dr. Cho, the doctor at Ilsan. I was pleased to learn that she, too, was bilingual in English and Korean. She asked when I had lived at Ilsan. When I said 1972, she told me that she would have been one of my doctors back then as she had worked there since 1961. She and I laughed about how some of the descriptions of me were written, including, "Even in long institutional life, fortunately, he has been brought up as such a nice boy without problem in personality."

I was amazed that Dr. Cho had stayed with Holt for so long. She revealed that she had actually tried, and managed, to retire several times. However, something kept calling her back to work with the kids. Impacting the lives of so many orphans throughout her career, she always found herself drawn back to help more children. I was deeply touched by her selfless nature and big heart. She is just the person needed by an orphan who is facing so much uncertainty and fear. I am so glad that she continues to be a part of Holt Ilsan after all these years.

Another exciting part of our visit was meeting one of the residents, a sweet little boy named Juno. He was three years old and needed help being fed by Molly and the volunteers while in the dining room. Molly told us that he had recently been transferred over to Ilsan after years with a foster mother because his many medical conditions made him harder and harder to be placed up for adoption. Juno was able to move his arms and legs easily, but was not allowed to walk on his own without support for fear that if he put too much weight down he may break bones in his feet. He had broken bones easily in the past, and further testing needed to be done to diagnose what medical needs he was facing. It broke my heart as I watched my daughter pick up the beach ball we had brought along and toss it back and forth with Juno. I held Juno on my lap as he laughed and wiggled, totally engaged in the fun of tossing and catching the ball with my daughter. I wondered why such an amazing, energetic little boy could be placed in a category as undesirable. My research had found that Korea is still not as advanced in tolerating people with special needs as we are in other countries, and that the laws there are still far behind in acknowledging the rights of disabled people. It made me sad to think that a country with such amazing advancements in technology, communication, and inventions could still be in the dark ages when it came to the rights of people with disabilities. I hope that this changes, for the sake of Juno and folks like him who long for a chance to be treated and valued as members of society.

The final part of our Ilsan visit consisted of a tour of the property, including the modern museum that was added to honor all the amazing work done by Harry and Bertha Holt. Harry had been only fifty-nine years old when he died in 1964. It was a shock not only to the Holt family, but to the orphans who grew up close to him under the loving care of Holt International, and who fondly called him "Grandpa." A memorial was built on the property at Islan orphanage to mark the graves of Harry and Bertha Holt. There are exactly fifty-nine steps leading up to the hilltop to the memorial to mark each year of Harry's short but impactful life. After his death, Bertha selflessly carried on the Holt mission on her own, always believing that all children should be loved without discrimination. Bertha died in 2000, but the legacy of Holt International still lives on through her daughter Molly and other family members, branching out into an organization that now helps orphans in twelve countries around the world, including China, India, Haiti, Ethiopia, and Vietnam.

Our tour guide was a nice young lady named Anna, who was very nervous about speaking English, especially after she learned my wife is an ESL teacher in the United States. It seems that although all Koreans are required to learn English while in school, many are reluctant to use it in conversing as they are more comfortable reading and writing it. My wife assured Anna that her English was perfectly understandable, which made Anna feel much more comfortable around us. She took us around the modest but spacious surroundings where I struggled to find a familiar spot. We passed several buildings, but Anna explained that most of the buildings had been remodeled or updated since 1972, so nothing really was the same as I had remembered. She remarked that one building that I may remember had been untouched, but was quite a way down the road from where we were. She asked if we really wanted to walk that far to see it. I only thought for a split second before I told her that I had come halfway around the world just to see my old surroundings, so I could certainly manage several hundred more yards!

Unfortunately, the building did not seem to be as familiar to me as I had hoped. Maybe it was not one that I had frequented much, or maybe not at all, but it was still one of the original untouched buildings that had marked my stay during my time at Holt Ilsan. Though the day was slightly cloudy, my spirits were aglow with the relief that no painful memories had surfaced during my visit. I had only happy memories from my past as an orphan at Holt Ilsan, and this visit rekindled the comfortable and secure feelings I had stored so well in my memory, if not so much the physical looks of the place itself.

As we made our way back to Molly's office, I spotted a big plastic and metal jungle gym on the side of the path, and I joked that I sure didn't remember that being there! I was happy to know that the precious children who were now living at Holt would have such a great playground.

Back at Molly's office, and upon reaching the end of our visit, I hugged Dr. Cho and Molly good-bye. I was lost in my thoughts as we headed out the gate. I was so glad that I had come back after all these years, but I was even gladder that Molly has allowed the true heart of the organization to carry on, and not let it get bogged down in bureaucracy. The compassionate care for the kids is still present at the forefront, and Molly and Dr. Cho renewed my faith in the belief that some good things never come to an end.

Molly Holt, me and Dr. Cho-July 10, 2012 at Holt Ilsan Center, South Korea.

Chapter 23

Crashing Back to Reality

Wednesday evening, as I was sitting in my hotel room back in Incheon after coming off of a remarkable and emotional reconnection at Holt Ilsan Center, I received the following email from Lucia at KBS TV:

Dear Mr. Stearns,

How are you? Thank you for your being so cooperative in filming for your story yesterday.

We have an important news to you.

I am very sorry to say but this program on July 13th will not be broadcast because KBS is a national enterprise and they decided to broadcast live confirmaton hearing for the appointment of Chief Justice of Supreme Court that are now being held during this weekdays at 11:00 am.

So your story will be broadcast on July 20th one week later.

We are very sorry about that.

I hope you will have a great time in Korea with your family and if you have any questions, feel free to call or email me. Take care.

With kind regards

Lucia

I was devastated. I had been focusing on the dream of broadcasting my story on Friday, July 13. That would allow a week for anyone to call in with information about my brothers before I had to go to back to America on July 21. With that kind of time on my side, it may have been possible for me to reunite with my brothers on the following show on July 20 so that I could actually meet them while I was still here in Korea. Now, I would not get the opportunity to even present my story to the Korean people until Friday, July 20. I figured that by the time anyone called in with information, I would be long gone on a plane back to America, and miss out on any chance of a reunion.

Luckily, one constant aspect of my personality is to not focus on things I cannot control. I think that was ingrained in me as a young child trying to survive each day, first with my brothers and no parents, and then later in the orphanage. I decided that being on the show on the twentieth was still a privilege, and that one broadcast could do more to spread the word about my situation than I could ever do on my own. I pushed down my disappointment and frustration and focused on the positives: I was still in Korea, closer to my Korean family than if I had never left America, and I still had the TV show coming up. Sometimes things happen the way they do for reasons we cannot understand, and it was not in my nature to dwell on the why's and how's. I concentrated on making the most of the next few days to explore Korea until I could be on the show.

Chapter 24

Busan

On Saturday, July 14, Carolyn, Elena, and I decided to make the journey down to Busan, the city of my birth. Although we were 215 miles away in Incheon, we had the luxury of Korea's technologically advanced transportation system. We could get to Busan in no time via the Korea Train eXpress, or KTX. This is a high speed railway train that could travel up to 217 miles per hour. We could leave Incheon in the morning, and arrive in Busan a short time later.

Since our daughter had been begging us to take her to a beach since the minute we arrived in South Korea, it was a perfect destination. We bought three tickets for the 10:10 KTX train to Busan, and after packing a small bag with our towels and swimsuits, we were on our way.

The train ride was as smooth as silk as we glided through the vast Korean countryside, past flowing rivers, thriving rice paddies, and spacious pastures. My wife and I held our breath at the cleanliness and beauty of the landscape around us. There was a feeling of serenity as the miles ticked forward, and it dawned on me how fitting a nickname was given to this majestic land: Land of the Morning Calm.

We arrived in Busan and exited the train. There was a light rain misting around us, but not enough to dissuade us and other like-minded beachgoers from enjoying the perfect beauty of Haeundae Beach. We were told as we exited the train station terminal that this would be the perfect beach to visit as it was only a short subway ride away, and it was the most famous beach in all of Korea.

On the beach, while my wife and daughter raced toward the waves, I stood with my hands on my hips and thought about where I was. I was in Busan, the city of my birth, half a world away from the place I had grown up in America. I slowly turned to look in all directions, and could not keep from wondering if my brothers were still here. Here, in Busan, where we had struggled so many long years ago to survive. I would not even begin to know where exactly our small hut would have stood, as the city around me now was so huge and contemporary. I hoped that my Korean family was still here, somewhere, and I hoped that they would welcome the thought of seeing me again. I had always known that we were separated at the train station, but one thing I had never really let myself think about was whether or not they thought much about me afterward. Maybe it made their lives easier to not have to worry about me, especially for Kyang Soo, who lost most of his childhood as he was thrust into the role of caretaker of two younger and demanding brothers.

* * *

The KTX ride back to Seoul was relaxing. I had spent a great afternoon at Haeundae Beach, and got to breathe in the same air that I imagined my brothers were breathing. It was great to finally be there, but at the same time, it was difficult because I kept wondering how close they were. As I walked along the beach, and later the streets of the city, I scanned faces absentmindedly. It probably would have not mattered much if my brothers had passed right by me, as so many years had gone by; I doubt that we would even recognize each other. I was glad that I was insistent with KBS that a photo of me as a child would be aired. Even though we had been separated for almost four years when the picture of me was taken as I was admitted into Holt Orphanage, it was the only photo I had from my youth. It was the closest thing I had to me looking the way I did when Kyang Soo and Yae Soo knew me, and I hoped that when the show aired, that one photo would be enough for them to realize that this full grown (and slightly gray-haired!) man on the screen was really their little brother.

* * *

On the morning of July 17, 2012, Gina called me at the hotel with excitement in her voice. Her brother Byeong-Su had called her after receiving a call from the police. They had told him that since there were hundreds of Kyang Soo's, it would be a difficult lead to follow. However, because of Yae Soo's unique name, they were able to narrow down the search for him to just two men who would have been born in the time frame that I had given. So the goal of the police was to try to track down Yae Soo, with the possibility that finding one brother would lead to finding the other one. I was once again full of hope that my dream of reuniting with my brothers could be a reality. However, with only three and a half days remaining of my trip, I didn't let the hope linger for long. The police had told me initially when I went to fill out the report that it could take ninety days or longer to find them, assuming they were even able to be found. I once again tried to put my emotions into check, as I had for the past week and a half of this journey. I felt in my heart that this was not going to be the time in my life that I would find them; I felt time was not going to be on my side. Since the rescheduling of my appearance on *I Miss That Person,* it seemed there would not be enough time for everything to happen. The new taping was airing on Friday, July 20 at 11:00 a.m., and my return flight back to the USA departed at 4:00 p.m. the next day. It did not seem like much time was left for my brothers to be located either by the show or the police station in enough time for me to meet them before I headed back on the long flight back to the USA. I had been in Korea for the past week and a half, and unless I heard something from the police before the show aired on Friday, everything would have to come down to the last 24 hours.

I decided right then that I had experienced more in this visit to Korea about my past, and about Korea itself, than I had ever dreamed, and I was happy about that. Maybe someday after I returned home to America, my phone would ring with either KBS or the police station calling to say they had found information about at least one of my brothers. Even if they were no longer alive, at least I could have some answers to put some closure on those chapters of my life. Once again, I took a backseat to what I could not control, and found the peace to move forward and live one day at a time. With that thought comforting me, I busied myself in trying to see and experience more of Korea's beautiful offerings in what little time I had left there.

We continued to spend time with Gina's large family, and their kindness and hospitality were endless. We drove to Yong Pyong to meet Gina's youngest sister, and stayed at a beautiful countryside hotel which many Korean families use as a getaway from the hustle and bustle of the large, crowded cities.

It was picturesque and relaxing, and we all stayed up late into the night, enjoying delicious Korean barbeque and singing karaoke in the nearby hotel lounge. My heart was light as I kept the thought of appearing on the TV show on Friday morning in the front of my mind. I realized that I was at a dead-end for information, and the show was my best route for finding the answers I desperately wanted.

Chapter 25

I Miss That Person

I awoke on Friday, July 20, the morning of the taping of the live show, with butterflies in my stomach. I was not so nervous about being on camera in front of millions of viewers as much as I was about telling my story. I was afraid of a repeat of that day at the train station when all the memories welled up inside me and I broke down in tears, and that I would once again have to relive the loss I had tried so hard through the years to suppress. It was getting harder to be in Korea, knowing that my brothers could very well be so close, yet we were still so far apart.

Carolyn, Elena, and I took a taxi to Seoul so that we could be at the KBS studio at nine o'clock. Lucia was going to meet us there to go over the script of questions that I would be asked during the live broadcast. As we sat in the cavernous cafeteria of the KBS building, I scanned the script. They were the same questions that I had been asked earlier via email, and focused mostly on how I came to be separated from my brother at the train station, and how my life had changed since then. As I read, I understood that this show was just going to focus on me telling my story. In the back of my mind, I had hoped that maybe my brothers had been located, and KBS would make this show into the reunion show I had hoped for when Lucia and I first started communicating via emails back in March. However, the more I read through the script, and when we were finally led to a green room to get last minute instructions and wait to be escorted onto the live stage, the more I knew that there were going to be no surprises. My brothers were not there. It was going to be me, up on stage, telling my story, and pleading with viewers to call the station if they had any information that could help me find my brothers. After I came to grips with the fact that I would not be reconnecting with anyone in my family that day, I focused on trying to squeeze in as many details as I could into the little time I would have on stage. The more details I could remember, the better my chances were that someone out there would be able to help.

Finally, at 10:45, we were led out of the green room and onto the small stage in front of a live audience. There were several other guests seated onstage who were presenting their stories as well. One woman had appeared on the show a couple weeks prior, and now was brought back to be reunited with her long lost sibling on this very episode. She was scheduled to appear before me, and I was to be given the last half hour of the show to present my story. I was nervous as I was led to the stage and shown where to stand when it was my turn to speak. To my wife's surprise, the stagehand led her to the stage to sit in one of the two empty seats in the first of two short rows reserved for guests appearing on the show. Carolyn had anticipated just sitting in the audience with our daughter and watching the show from there. Elena was instead escorted by Lucia to sit in the audience beside her so that both Carolyn and I could be on the stage. Neither Carolyn nor I thought too much into this at the time.

We waited quietly as the cameraman counted down, and a light began blinking to signal us that we were now live on the air. I was seated in the front row, first seat on the left, with Carolyn directly on my right. The show's theme music started playing, the hosts began speaking in Korean, and the next half an hour became a blur. I listened to the hosts and the first guest speaking about her situation, but try as I might, I could not understand enough Korean to follow what was going on. I could only watch the cues of the audience and the other guests around me to know when to clap and smile. Finally, near the end of her segment, the long-lost relative of the first guest was brought out for their reunion. It was a touching moment, and brought tears to my eyes. I couldn't help but wonder if I would ever be lucky enough to experience that moment when someone you have been away from for so long was finally there beside you. I didn't even know how I would act in that situation. It turned out I would not have any more time to think about it. It was my turn; this was my moment.

Chapter 26

Praying for a Miracle

I feel there have been so many events that have happened in my life that could not have happened merely by chance, starting with my separation from my family at the Seoul Train Station in 1968, to the events that led me to two different orphanages in Korea, and finally to the unusual way I was adopted to America when I was older and unlikely to ever get adopted. I have often felt my life was heading in a direction that was beyond my control. I sometimes felt like I was being guided to just go with the flow and not to worry, because I would always be taken care of. Maybe this was due to the deep faith I had that God would always protect me, and maybe it was partly just easier to let God do the driving while I sat in the passenger seat during the times when I was clearly in over my head. I learned from an early age not to stress over things that I could not control, but to work hard to change the things that *were* in my control, like trying to fit in when I was new to America and needed to learn a new language, culture, and bond with strangers to make a new family. I knew when to step aside and follow God's lead, like when I decided to come to Korea for the first time since I left as a little boy. I had many doubts about coming back, due to not wanting to take time off when I just started working at a new company, as well as not being sure it was the right time for me to just pack up and go back to the past. I didn't know if I was emotionally ready to open myself up to what I may find if it was going to be unpleasant. Sometimes it was easier to just let things keep going along as they were since I was comfortable in my life, and not try to stir things up that could disrupt that comfort level. But then I kept thinking back to how my father Frank had died so suddenly, and I how I needed to view that as a wake-up call and realize that nothing in life was ever truly comfortable. His death was what spurred me to stop wasting time about finding the answers I longed for about my brothers. I knew I had needed to make this trip whether I felt 100% ready to or not, and that God would decide what the outcome would be, not me.

God can be very persistent. I had many reservations of whether it was a good idea to open the Pandora's Box of my past. My ultimate decision was to put it into God's hands, and let Him guide me in the direction I was supposed to go, as He had so many times before in my life.

So, as I took my place at the podium, live on the stage of *I Miss That Person* on July 20, 2012, at 11:30 a.m., I realized that this was it. This was what I had been anticipating, fearing, and longing for all my life. I was going to tell my story to the world, and let the cards fall where they may. Whatever answers I may find, I knew that they were just part of my story, for good or for bad, and I was ready to learn the rest, if God meant for me to learn it. A KBS interpreter named Helen was standing beside me to translate my English words into Korean so that the audience of millions of viewers in Korea, as well as the hosts of the show, could understand me. A brief introductory video was played of my wife, daughter, and I spending our first days in Korea. It showed our arrival at Incheon airport, as well as my visit to Holt Post-Adoption Services, and my emotional visit to the old Seoul Train Station. All of the many hours of footage taken by the KBS camera crew over three days were condensed into a concise three-minute introduction to my past. While I watched it, I could feel the tears welling up in my eyes again, especially when I saw myself for the first time crying in the train station in the exact spot where I was separated forever from my Korean family. I held back the tears, and when prompted by the hosts, in a choked voice, I began to tell my story.

Helen and I at the podium at KBS studio live on I Miss That Person—July 20, 2012.

Through Helen, I answered questions from the hosts. I spoke about how I became lost at the train station, what I remembered about my time in the orphanages, and what my life was like after I was adopted and brought to

America. All through the interview, I was praying that someone out there would recognize me or my story, and call in with some information about my brothers. I was intent on telling my story clearly so that no details would get lost in translation. The more information the public had, the better chance *I* had of finding my brothers again. I was so preoccupied with telling my story, that what happened next completely caught me off guard.

Chapter 27

Saving the Best for Last

After I finished talking about my career in America, the hosts began talking to each other in Korean. While my Korean language skills were old and rusty, I could just make out a little of what they were discussing. It sounded like they said "one brother here" and "TV station." Anxiously, I looked at Helen. She interpreted what I had been waiting to hear my entire life. The hosts were telling her that my brothers had been found and one of them was backstage waiting right now!

I could not believe what I was hearing. I asked her a couple times if they were there, right now, to make sure I heard right. Yes, she confirmed, and her words were music to my ears. "Which brother?" I asked, figuring it would be Yae Soo, since I knew that there had been a better chance of locating him because of his unusual name. When Helen said it was Kyang Soo, I was completely speechless. The last person I ever expected to track down was Kyang Soo. Looking for him, with such a common name (like the American equivalent of John Smith) was like finding a needle in a haystack. My heart was pounding as the hosts asked me to step out from behind the podium and move toward the stage door to call for my brother to come out. Still in a state of shock, and not quite believing this was really happening, I softly called his name. The hosts and Helen prompted me to call his name louder, so I collected myself and managed to call out slightly louder, "Kyang

Soo." What I saw next was such an amazing sight, accompanied by so many unresolved emotions, that is hard to put into words.

Walking toward me, after forty-four years apart, was Kyang Soo. My brother. My hero. My protector when I was just a young child. I walked toward his outstretched arms and embraced him in a hug that felt so warm and complete. It was him. It was Kyang Soo, and he was here. My brother, from whom I had been cruelly separated that one fateful day in Seoul Train Station, was here and holding me in his arms, afraid to let go again. I felt the same way. Nothing could have prepared me for this moment in my life. Even if the producers at KBS would have told me of this surprise beforehand, I don't know if I would have believed it then either. Reuniting with Kyang Soo after living most of my life halfway across the world was something I believed would never come to pass.

When we finally let go of each other, there were so many questions that I needed to ask. How did KBS find him? What happened at the train station, and what did he and the family do after I was lost? Did he know where Yae Soo was? What happened to my Korean mom and dad? Luckily, with the help of Helen, these questions were finally answered.

Kyang Soo said that he and Yae Soo did stay together after I disappeared. Yae Soo lived close by him now in our hometown of Busan, and was actually driving up from there to meet us here at the KBS station as we spoke. I found out later that Kyang Soo had received a call from KBS the previous evening. They asked him some general questions about an incident that happened at the Seoul Train Station in 1968, and Kyang Soo quickly confirmed the story, and gave even more details. While the station was sure that Kyang Soo was the right person, they only told him that "they may have found your youngest brother," but that it was not definitely confirmed. After all, it would be more tragic to have him come to the show and meet me only to find out I was not actually the right person. So, while KBS was pretty certain they had a match, they needed to be cautious. They told Kyang Soo they would call him later that evening and let him know if he needed to come to Seoul to be on the show on Friday morning or not. Kyang Soo packed a small bag just in case. Since Busan was 200 miles from Seoul, where the KBS station was located, they would have to take the KTX train to be able to make it in time for the live show. Finally, at two a.m., Kyang Soo got the call he had been waiting for since my disappearance so many years ago. KBS wanted him to come to the station and sit backstage while the live show was taping. They were pretty sure a guest scheduled to appear on the show could be his long lost brother, and needed him to watch from backstage while the show was taping to confirm his identity before they could be introduced.

Kyang Soo could not sleep. A week earlier he had had vivid dreams that woke him up in a sweat. The dreams were of me and him when we were young again. He thought it was odd that for the whole week he would have the same dreams of me night after night.

After the call came from KBS, he tossed and turned and cried all night. He felt exactly as I did. Just the thought that we could be reunited after all this time was emotional enough, and he did not even know how he would act if it all was true, and I turned out to really be Ji Soo. He called Yae Soo, and told Yae Soo the news. Since Yae Soo had work that he did in Seoul, and was driving up there anyway in the morning, he would meet us there after the show aired to reunite with me if I really turned out to be who I said I was. They still couldn't be sure at this point, no more than I could be sure that they were not some strangers just claiming to be my family for whatever reasons anyone would do that. Carolyn and I even joked before we came to Korea that maybe we should require a DNA test before we got all excited that we really found my brothers because how would I know it was them? I hadn't seen them in years, and we sure would not look the same as we had when we were together. I did not have any photos of them as kids; I only had images of them locked in my memory to rely on.

However, when Kyang Soo was backstage watching me speaking as the show was airing live, he broke down in tears. He knew it instantly. It was me, Ji Soo. There was no doubt whatsoever in his mind. Not only did my story match what he knew, but after one look at my face, it was undeniable that we shared the same genes. At the same time he was backstage, his cell phone was ringing off the hook with relatives calling him and telling him to turn on the show *I Miss That Person* because Ji Soo was on there! They did not have any idea that he was backstage and ready to come out in a matter of seconds to finally see me face to face after all those years.

As I called his name for the final time, he was directed to open the door and come out to the stage. He needed no prompting, as he had waited for this day to come for as long as I had, maybe even more so, as I would later find out. He was holding a photo of our Korean mother, and I saw I was the spitting image of her. I resembled her so much; it was like looking in a mirror. As I looked at the photo of our mother, I knew no DNA test was necessary.

This was my family. This was my brother. After all this time, across all the miles, we finally found each other.

Chapter 28

Getting to Know You

My dream had come true. I had found my brother Kyang Soo. Then, two hours after the show's end, my prayers were answered again when I met my second brother, Yae Soo. Carolyn, Elena, Kyang Soo, his beautiful wife Mi Kyoung, and I all walked across the street to a nearby restaurant. There, heading down the street toward us was Yae Soo. He had just arrived in Seoul after making the long trip from Busan, and stopped in his tracks when he saw me. I could tell from the look on his face that he was just as emotional as I felt. We embraced in a hug, and no words were needed. His face looked so much like mine that there was no doubt he was my middle brother. We hugged for a while as we enjoyed the miracle of being reunited after all those years apart.

Our biggest challenge was communicating. My brothers and their families didn't speak English and my family didn't speak Korean, so it was wonderful that KBS allowed Helen to come with us to interpret while we reconnected after all that time. She explained that part of her role besides translating was to act as a counselor to help families transition with the major changes in their lives when reconnecting with their past. She said that a lot of reunions are filled with resentment and hard feelings, and it can be a difficult time for both families. She was pleasantly surprised to find out how much all of our families had been waiting for this day to happen. There were no hard feelings with any of us, just pure joy.

Helen was amazing as she patiently translated the many questions we all had for each other about what had really happened that day in the train station and all the years afterwards. We all had so many questions, and finally, after all the pieces of the story were put together, we had what we had all been searching for in our hearts and minds: closure.

Chapter 29

Answers

I had often felt as if my life was a book with the middle filled in, but with so many pages missing from the beginning. I know my brothers had felt the same way after I disappeared from their lives. What I had never anticipated, though, was how deep their suffering was. Kyang Soo developed stomach cancer last year after a life of worrying about me and the guilt that came with it. He spent many years trying to find solace in a bottle of alcohol. Yae Soo and Kyang Soo never remained close, and I could not help but wonder if my disappearance had driven a wedge between them, as I'm certain blame and guilt were passed around among the family members.

From what Kyang Soo told Helen, and what I could piece together through her translation, the missing pages were slowly and painfully filled in:

Our mother and father were well-liked members of one of the small villages that was then Busan. I was the youngest of three brothers, born to them on July 3, 1961. After my birth, my parents starting drifting apart. My father was a clerk in the court, a prestigious job at the time, and left my mother when I was very small to move to Seoul to be near another woman. My mother, still young and beautiful, took on many jobs to try to support us. She worked hard to make sure we would not lose our modest home. But without my father there, it was a difficult time for a single mother, and she was never able to be home much. That is why I do not remember my parents, and what I did remember was only their constant fighting with each other.

At one point, my mother decided to go to Seoul to try to talk to my father about coming back home to his family. That is when I remember Kyang Soo taking care of Yae Soo and me. As the oldest brother in the family, it now became his duty to take care of the family. At the time, he was still a child himself. After some time, my mother returned so that she could take us up to Seoul to stay with some relatives. Things were not working out well for her to be able to work and keep us in Busan, so we needed to move. I was six at the time, and Kyang Soo was twelve.

We were taken to a relative's house to stay. Kyang Soo said that I always cried to go back home to Busan. I did not want to stay there, and made it no secret to anyone. Kyang Soo decided to get a job shining shoes at the nearby Seoul train station. With the money he earned, he planned to save enough to buy three train tickets back to Busan. None of us was happy, and he wanted us to go back home to the village where we were more familiar, to what we had always called home.

On one particular morning, after Kyang Soo had just arrived for work at the train station, he turned around to find me standing behind him. He was surprised that I had managed to quietly follow him without his knowing. He told me to go back to the relative's house and stay with Yae Soo. I argued with him and told him I did not like it there and I wanted to go home NOW! Running out of patience with my six-year-old defiance, Kyang Soo yelled that I needed to go back to the house and wait for him there. He would come and get me later, and then we would talk about what to do. He was not comfortable at the relative's house, and he had found another place to stay. He said I still needed to stay with the relatives until he had enough money for the tickets, then he would come back and get Yae Soo and me and we could go back home to Busan.

Finally, I grew tired of being yelled at, and agreed with his plan for me to go back to the relative's house. Kyang Soo, now very late for work, did not have time to walk me back. He asked if I remembered how to get back to the house by myself and I lied and said "Yes." I was afraid to admit I did not remember because he was very angry, and I did not want to make him any angrier. He told me to go then and be on my way, and after he walked away, that was the last time we saw each other.

The train station was so crowded with people hurrying to catch their trains, and I did not know what to do. I forgot how to get back, but had been too afraid to tell Kyang Soo. So I did what any six-year-old would likely do in that situation: I hid under the closest bench and cried. I knew from there how the rest of my life went, but I never knew what happened to Kyang Soo and the rest of my family.

It was over a year before anyone had realized I was missing. It is hard to imagine, but that was back in a time when Korea was still pretty rural, and telephones and modern communication systems were scarce. My brother left the train station that day after work assuming that I had safely made my way back home to the relative's house. Meanwhile, the relatives had assumed I had gone off to work with Kyang Soo, and was also staying at the new place he was staying at now. My mother and father were still somewhere else in Seoul and did not know what was happening with their children.

When it was finally realized that I had never come back from the train station that day, panic set in for all of my family. I can only imagine the blame, guilt, and hurt feelings that passed among them as they tried to make sense of how something like that could have happened. Unknown to them, I was now living as an orphan at Hwa Saeng Won. Kyang Soo said they searched everywhere but I had simply just disappeared. No one could find a trace of me. There were so many orphanages around the area after the Korean War that they did not have the resources to cover them all. And because I did not enter Hwa Saeng Won through a police station as was customary and proper, there was no way for the police to trace me. I was gone, without a trace, and with no clues as to where I could be. Even worse, a year had gone by, so anything could have happened to me with so much time wasted.

But Kyang Soo never stopped searching. He was so sick with guilt that he had not protected his littlest brother. Yae Soo was okay this whole time, having stayed at the relative's house like he was supposed to do. Finally, Kyang Soo heard around to try looking at Holt Orphanage. However, by the time he got that information and went to Holt, they confirmed that I had indeed been staying there, but unfortunately I was already gone. Kyang Soo, although relieved to hear that I was still alive, was devastated. I had been adopted to America, and was now 6,000 miles away. Holt had a firm policy not to give out any information about a closed adoption, and so at that point the records were sealed. The trail ended. Once again, I was gone.

* * *

I also learned more sad news about my biological parents. It turns out that my father, Kim Tae Hee, had left my mother and moved in with another woman in Seoul. That is why my mother, Ahn Kyu Soo, went up to Seoul to try to get him to return to the family. He never returned to our family, and Kyang Soo said that he later tracked our mother down in Busan again shortly after he learned I became missing at the train station. She had no house and no money, so Kyang Soo took care of her for the rest of his life. Kim Tae Hee came back down to Busan once when Kyang Soo was nineteen to see if Kyang Soo was going to stay in Busan or come back up to Seoul to be closer to him. It was a shock to him to hear that I had been adopted to America. All this time, both he and my mother thought that I was with the other parent.

I asked Kyang Soo who the woman was who came to Holt Orphanage so many years ago claiming that she was a relative of mine. He thought that it was the woman that my dad had left my mom to be with. For some reason, the family had always believed she knew where I was, but that she had lost contact with my father, and never let anyone in my family know that I was in the orphanage. Back in 1972, she told me that I had an uncle in the military, and that turned out to be true. My father's brother was a general in the army, Kyang Soo confirmed. Kyang Soo also said that at one point, the family believed that she was the one who had put me in the orphanage, but none of that was true. This information was startling to me. Maybe if I had gone with her, I would have been reunited with my Korean family then, and not have ended up living in America with a new family.

Kyang Soo said that after he told my mother that I had disappeared, they went to Holt to see if they would give her any more information about my adoption. However, back then, international adoption was a very difficult process, and they were given no more information. According to Kyang Soo, my mother blamed herself for what had happened to me, and never fully got over the guilt she felt for not taking better care of us. According to Kyang Soo, she was a very good person, and just had a lot of hard things happening at the time when we were so young, and she never forgave herself for how things turned out.

Kyang Soo and my mother returned to live in Busan, where more of her and my father's family were still living, and that's where they stayed from then on. Yae Soo, who had still been in Seoul, came back to Busan a few years later when he needed to get an ID card of some sort, and ended up living back in Busan again; however, my brothers did not stay close to each other anymore and were both very busy with their lives.

* * *

My flight back to the US was scheduled to leave at 4:00 p.m. the next day. However, there was no doubt in my mind that I was not ready to head back yet. I had just found my brothers again, and my lifelong dream of a reunion was realized. I called the airlines and arranged for my family and me to stay for one more week so that I could spend time reconnecting with my newfound family. Kyang Soo and Yae Soo informed me that I had many, many relatives who had been longing to see me all those years, and as a matter of fact, I had over 200 cousins alone! I went from knowing no one in Korea to having an amazingly large family in a matter of minutes! The week was planned for me to travel to different parts of Korea with Kyang Soo and Mi Kyoung to meet all the long lost relatives from both my father and mother's side. However, my first visit was the most important one. On Saturday morning, Helen accompanied me, my wife, daughter, Kyang Soo, and Mi Kyoung on the 10:10 KTX to Busan. When Carolyn, Elena, and I made this same trip a little over a week earlier, it was only a dream that I would ever find my brothers. As I recalled standing on Haeundae Beach and wondering if they were still in Busan, I was amazed to now learn that Kyang Soo and Mi Kyoung lived less than ten minutes from the exact spot where I had stood. And now, here I was, making the same trip back to Busan, sitting beside none other than Kyang Soo in the flesh. It was all so surreal to me, and thankfully Helen was there to translate as my brother and I passed questions and answers back and forth in our different languages. We had so much time to make up, so much to learn, and so much to rejoice in. Kyang Soo and I realized how much we had in common, and discovered that we both had such an easygoing attitude and sense of humor. When Kyang Soo learned I wanted to write a book about my life, he said to make sure to make him "the handsome one"!

Our first stop once we got to Busan was to visit my Korean mother in the hospital where she had been a patient for the past six years. She had fallen ill and was in a coma state, unable to communicate. While her eyes were open, they would wander aimlessly left, right, up, and down, without having much real focus. I could only pray that as Kyang Soo placed my hand in hers and repeated to her eagerly over and over that "Ji Soo had come home," that there was some understanding reaching into her that would allow her mind to finally be at ease. Kyang Soo told me that she had suffered and blamed herself so much for my disappearance that she could never "close her eyes" until she knew what had ever become of me. I had hoped that my brief visit was enough to give her the peace that she needed to forgive herself and release her earthly burdens. I wanted to let her know that I turned out great, and it was because of her sacrifice that I was able to have a most fulfilling life in America, even though it was not how any of us would have planned in 1968.

As I looked at her beautiful face and marveled over the close family resemblance that I could plainly see, I could have sworn I felt a small squeeze from her tiny hand. It was only slight, and very fleeting, but enough so that I did notice. My one regret is that I had not been drawn sooner to come back and look for my biological family. How I would have loved to have met her, and enjoyed spending time getting to know her. Now that I had come back, it was too late, as she and my father would not know that I was truly all right all those long years they had suffered.

* * *

Our second stop in Busan was to visit the mausoleum where my father was entombed. Because land is so scarce in Korea, it is not used for cemeteries like the sprawling fields of green we are used to in the United States. It was coincidental to learn that my Korean father died in 2009, the same year that my American father had. Kim Tae Hee had died in September due to heart trouble. Kyang Soo said that after my Korean father had learned I had disappeared, he faithfully watched *I Miss That Person* every week, always hoping that one day I would appear on the show looking to find my long-lost family. How sad I felt upon learning that. I had been living comfortably in

America, with no thoughts whatsoever that my biological family was suffering so much over me.

I learned that both my brothers and their wives' names were engraved on my father's stone at his grave. There was a blank spot left intentionally under their names, and they explained to me why: they had always hoped to find me again, and when they did, my name and my wife's would be added to complete the family legacy. Yae Soo, Kyang Soo, and I were all emotional and embraced each other tightly as we realized that we were finally all together. We had found each other after so long and against so many obstacles, and knew we would never let anything come between us again.

Yae Soo, 53, Jin Soo, 50, and Kyang Soo, 56, visiting father Kim Tae Hee's grave at Busan Memorial Park, Busan, South Korea.

Chapter 30

Then and Now

I returned to America on July 28, 2012, after having spent almost a week reconnecting with my long-lost Korean family. I had relatives from both my Korean mother's and father's sides of the family eager to see me again after all those years. I met aunts, uncles and cousins who remembered me and knew me as that little boy before I had gone missing at the train station. They told me of how the family had longed to find me for all those years and had never given up hope that one day I would be found alive. It was hard to comprehend then, and still is, that I had so many people in Korea aching for my return during all those years when I had thought no one cared about me.

Once home again in America, I vowed to never lose touch again with my brothers, and to do whatever I could to break through the language barrier. My wife, daughter and I enrolled in Korean language lessons through a nearby Korean church so we could try to learn the language that I knew so fluently as a child, but was now out of reach when I needed it. We set up Skype on our computer; Kyang Soo did the same on his, and we have spent many hours "together," writing basic words in Korean and English back and forth to show each other how we are trying to learn about the other's language. Even though we can't say much yet, just being able to see each other and smile and laugh together via the computer screen is so fulfilling and warms both our hearts. We had never thought the day would come that we would meet again in this world, so in every minute we can connect we relive the miracle that we experienced on July 20th, 2012. I have made plans to go back and visit later in 2013, and am excited to meet all the relatives and friends I did not have a chance to meet on my first trip.

People often ask how I feel after discovering so many details about my unknown past. I don't think there are words in any language that can really answer that. I guess the closest word that comes to mind is "bittersweet." Although I have the answers I sought, I cannot say if I have opened up wounds that were better left closed.

For example, I think it is glorious and amazing that I now have two families, one biological in Korea, and one through adoption in the United States. I feel proud to have experiences from two amazing cultures influencing my actions. I realized early on I could overcome barriers in language, and learned how to continually persevere in the face of discrimination. I became a strong person mentally and emotionally, and I honestly feel I would not want to change a minute of my past. To alter any one piece in my life story would wear away at my character, and I don't think I would be who I am today.

I don't know if both of my families will truly understand how I would not want to change my past. True, I wish that my biological parents and brothers did not have to suffer all those years not knowing what had happened to me. I know now that they had so much pain in their lives after I was lost, and I regret that they had that. But I know in my heart that it was God's plan for my life to be led into a different family in a foreign land. I was so young when I was separated from my biological family that I was able to bury my own pain, and allow for my survival instinct to kick in. While I was in the orphanages, I did not have time to miss anyone because I was so busy trying to cope with, and make sense of, my new life. By the time I found out I had been adopted and was going to live in America, I had pretty much resigned myself to the fact that I was no longer meant to live in Korea, and a new world would be opened up to me in America.

I cannot say if my life would be better or worse had I never gotten lost. No one can do anything more than speculate with that sort of situation. Out of great respect for the suffering of my biological family, I will never say that I am glad that it happened. However, I *can* say that I am alright that it happened. Otherwise, I would not have been raised by Frank and Pat Stearns, nor would I have made the valuable friendships and memories that I did by living in Greenville, Pennsylvania. I grew up with the influence of two cultures, first from my early years in Korea, then in my later years in America. Because of the rich diversity of these cultures, I am able to be the unique individual that I am today. The people I have come across in both countries have all played a role in shaping my views, attitudes, and sense of self. I think if I would change even one tiny piece of the puzzle, I would not be the way I am today.

And through all the trials and tribulations, joy and glory, I know who I am.

I am Jin Soo Stearns, and that is my story.

Kyang Soo and I in July, 2012 standing in front of the Old Seoul Railroad station where I became lost 44 years earlier after following him there.